THE
1990s

Other books in this series:

THE

1990s

Stuart A. Kallen, *Book Editor*

David L. Bender, *Publisher*
Bruno Leone, *Executive Editor*
Bonnie Szumski, *Series Editor*
David M. Haugen, *Managing Editor*

Greenhaven Press, Inc., San Diego, California

AMERICA'S DECADES

Every effort has been made to trace the owners of copyrighted material. The articles in this volume may have been edited for content, length, and/or reading level. The titles have been changed to enhance the editorial purpose.

Library of Congress Cataloging-in-Publication Data

The 1990s / Stuart A. Kallen, book editor.
    p.   cm. — (America's decades)
  Includes bibliographical references and index.
  ISBN 0-7377-0312-1 (lib. bdg. : alk. paper) —
  ISBN 0-7377-0311-3 (pbk. : alk. paper)
    1. United States—Civilization—1990–2. 2. Nineteen
  nineties. I. Kallen, Stuart A., 1955–   . II. Series.

  E169.12 .A176 2000
  973.929—dc21   99-049999
                                                       CIP

Cover photo: 1. Reuters/Clay McLachlan/Archive Photos 2. AP/Photo
Agricultural Research Service—USDA, 171, 177
Library of Congress, 17

©2000 by Greenhaven Press, Inc.
P.O. Box 289009, San Diego, CA 92198-9009

Printed in the U.S.A.

Contents

Chapter 1: Politics and Policy in Washington

1. Bill Clinton Wins the White House

From the Health Security Plan to welfare reform and from Monica Lewinsky to the war in the former Yugoslavia, President Bill Clinton's two terms in office were anything but ordinary. Yet the president's popularity remained high as most Americans prospered during the nineties.

2. Clinton Survives Impeachment *by Kenneth T. Walsh*

Clinton's affair with Monica Lewinsky dominated everything from newspaper headlines to late-night comedy monologues for more than a year. Although Republicans in the House voted to impeach the president, they were not supported by the majority of the American public or the two-thirds of the Senate needed to remove Clinton from office.

3. Perot's Reform Party Continues Its Success

Ross Perot's Reform Party had almost disappeared by 1998 until former World Wrestling Federation superstar Jesse "the Body" Ventura was elected governor of Minnesota under the Reform Party banner. The election of such an outside-the-mainstream candidate speaks volumes about voter discontent in America.

Chapter 2: War and Peace After the Cold War

1. Eastern Europe Awakens to Freedom

After living under Communist dictatorships for decades, the collapse of the Soviet Union offered freedom and democracy to the nations of Eastern Europe for the first time since the end of World War II.

Is American culture responsible for creating a new generation of cold-blooded teenage killers?

Chapter 4: Racial and Gender Conflicts

Chapter 5: Pop Goes the Culture

Human Genome Project, scientists were mapping and identifying all of the estimated fifty thousand to one hundred thousand human genes on human DNA, discovering new genes and the roles they played in disease, and testing for the presence of genes that make people sick.

Foreword

In his book *The American Century*, historian Harold Evans maintains that the history of the twentieth century has been dominated by the rise of the United States as a global power: "The British dominated the nineteenth century, and the Chinese may cast a long shadow on the twenty-first, but the twentieth century belongs to the United States." In a 1998 interview he summarized his sweeping hypothesis this way: "At the beginning of the century the number of free democratic nations in the world was very limited. Now, at the end of the century, democracy is ascendant around the globe, and America has played the major part in making that happen."

As the new century dawns, historians are eager to appraise the past one hundred years. Evans's book is just one of many attempts to assess the historical impact that the United States has had in the past century. Although not all historians agree with Evans's characterization of the twentieth century as "America's century," no one disputes his basic observation that "in only the second century of its existence the United States became the world's leading economic, military and cultural power." For most of the twentieth century the United States has played an increasingly larger role in shaping world events. The Greenhaven Press America's Decades series is designed to help readers develop a better understanding of America and Americans during this important time.

Each volume in the ten-volume series provides an in-depth examination of the time period. In compiling each volume, editors have striven to cover not only the defining events of the decade—in both the domestic and international arenas—but also the cultural, intellectual, and technological trends that affected people's everyday lives.

Essays in the America's Decades series have been chosen for their concise, accessible, and engaging presentation of the facts. Each selection is preceded by a summary of the article's content. A comprehensive index and an annotated table of contents also aid readers in quickly locating material of interest. Each volume begins with an introductory essay that presents the broader themes of each decade. Several research aids are also present, including an extensive bibliography and a timeline that provides an at-a-glance overview of each decade.

Each volume in the Greenhaven Press America's Decades series serves as an informative introduction to a specific period in U.S. history. Together, the volumes comprise a detailed overview of twentieth century American history and serve as a valuable resource for students conducting research on this fascinating time period.

Introduction

Daily news events are, by their very definition, unexpected, hence the name *news*. Taken at face value after the fact, however, the outcome of such news events may be predictable or expected. But in the 1990s, reality and the perception of reality often took radically divergent paths. The impeachment of President Bill Clinton is a good example. Millions of Americans expected that the president's affair with a White House intern would quickly drive him from office. Instead, after weathering impeachment and trial in the Senate, the reality was that Clinton continued to emerge with record-high public approval ratings. A few powerful Republicans who strongly supported the president's removal, such as Speaker of the House Newt Gingrich and Congressman Bob Livingston were forced to resign instead. Anyone betting on what appeared to be the obvious outcome would have lost.

This theme was repeated in many other instances throughout the decade: The fall of the Soviet Union and the end of the Cold War did not end oppression in Eastern Europe or make the region more prosperous or peaceful. While some countries were able to make the transition to democracy, the former republics of the Soviet Union fell into economic chaos and political corruption that rivaled the misery of the Soviet system.

Although times change, people do not. The articles chosen for this anthology demonstrate that many of the issues that confronted people in the 1990s, while often unpredictable or unexpected, also challenged people in the past. Issues such as war, racial friction, moral questions posed by new technology, and the big questions of life and death were the same in the 1990s as they were fifty years ago. And as they will, no doubt, be fifty years hence.

As journalist Greil Marcus writes, "A decade . . . is nothing more than a piece of commodified time, moments erased and reshaped into something an infinite number of people can . . . [believe] simultaneously."[1]

Yet history, especially recent history, is not set in stone or a dead thing from the past. Rather, it is the living manifestation that shaped the world all of us live in today. The ideals, troubles, and good times of the interactive nineties will remain alive and relevant well into the twenty-first century.

1. Greil Marcus, "Kurt Cobain: Artist of the Decade," *Rolling Stone*, May 13, 1999, p. 47.

CHAPTER 1

Politics and Policy in Washington

AMERICA'S DECADES

head of the Democratic ticket, then threw geographical, political, and generational balance aside and named fellow baby
boomer Senator Albert Gore of Tennessee as his running
mate, proudly explaining that "There's a little Bubba in both
of us." The contest was complicated by the self-financed
third-party candidacy of eccentric billionaire industrialist H.
Ross Perot, who ran on a vague platform of balancing the
federal budget while opposing government in general.

Clinton was an entirely new kind of national Democrat:
a self-described moderate who had founded the utterly
middle-of-the-road Democratic Leadership Council. . . . He
also promised to cut the defense budget, provide tax relief
for the middle class, and offer a massive economic aid
package to the republics of the former Soviet Union. Witty
and intelligent, Clinton reminded some Democrats of JFK,
although not just in the good sense. During the campaign
whispers about Clinton's constant womanizing would be
voiced aloud by Gennifer Flowers, who claimed to have
had a twelve-year affair with the then-governor of
Arkansas. In addition, Clinton earned the nickname "Slick
Willie" for his inconsistency on some issues, his pandering
to special interest groups, and his carefully constructed responses to reporters' questions about his avoidance of the
Vietnam draft and his collegiate marijuana use, which he
tried to explain away by saying he "didn't inhale."

Perhaps due to overconfidence, Bush ran a sloppy and
surprisingly unprofessional campaign, foolishly relying on
his foreign-policy successes when the American people
were far more concerned with the economy, the deficit, and
the president's apparent lack of a credible domestic program; as colorful Clinton campaign adviser James Carville
kept stressing to his own staff, "It's the economy, stupid."
Apparently it was: Clinton won the 1992 election with 43
percent of the popular vote to Bush's 38 percent and Perot's
19 percent, and took the electoral college from Bush by
370 to 168 votes with none for Perot. Clinton's victory was
clear, but whether he had a mandate was debatable; if anything, the election of such an utter centrist indicated that

the nation was evolving beyond partisan politics to an even clearer emphasis on economic concerns.

Nevertheless, President Clinton set out an ambitious agenda for his first administration, the centerpiece of which was a comprehensive overhaul of the nation's health-care system. Early in 1993 he named his influential—some would say too powerful—wife, fellow Yale-educated lawyer Hillary

President Bill Clinton

Rodham Clinton, to chair a task force to study the situation and come up with recommendations for improving it. This appointment was a new twist for the American presidency, although the nation's history was full of strong first ladies, from Abigail Adams to Eleanor Roosevelt and more recently even more influential ones such as Rosalynn Carter and Nancy Reagan. None of them, however, had ever exercised real power in as official a fashion as Hillary Rodham Clinton.

After some months of serious investigation and debate, the health-care task force came up with a complicated and confusing set of programs that were immediately opposed by liberals and conservatives alike, upon which the commission released a series of compromise proposals that only muddied the matters further. In the end the Clintons abandoned their attempt to install the most comprehensive national health-care reforms since the Johnson administration, and under a heavy barrage of criticism Mrs. Clinton opted for a lower public profile.

Other initiatives also fell short of success during the early Clinton years. Several of the president's nominees for cabinet posts were either rejected or forced to step down before their confirmation votes. Clinton's efforts to end the ban on gays and lesbians serving in the U.S. armed forces resulted in a compromise policy called "Don't ask, don't tell" that angered those on both sides of the issue. Most damning, congressional investigations were launched into the Clintons' involvement in a complicated Arkansas land-speculation deal, given the umbrella designation "White-water," which the Republicans quickly dubbed "Whitewa-tergate" to add to the whiff of scandal about it. In a

The President's Plan for Health Care Reform

By the time Bill Clinton was elected in 1992, the number of Americans without health insurance had grown to 37 million. Unchecked federal health-care costs—25 percent of the federal budget—were expected to triple by 2030. Health care costs in 1994 made about 14 percent of the total American economy, and that number was expected to climb to 20 percent by 2000. The excerpt below, written by the White House Domestic Policy Council, spells out the details of Clinton's failed health care plan.

Universal Access: Every American citizen and legal resident should have access to health care without financial or other barriers.

Comprehensive Benefits: Guaranteed benefits should meet the full range of health needs, including primary, preventive and specialized care.

Choice: Each consumer should have the opportunity to exercise effective choice about providers, plans and treatments. Each consumer should be informed about what is known and not known about the risks and benefits of available treatments and be free to choose among them according to his and her preferences.

Fair Distribution of Costs: The health care system should spread the costs and burdens of care across the entire community, nutshell, Whitewater centered on allegations that Bill and Hillary Clinton might have received special treatment and the forgiveness of unsavory loans after the failure of their 1978 investment in a resort project on the White River in northern Arkansas. It didn't help that White House files were found listing Republicans who were being investigated in a systematic way that smacked of Richard Nixon's notorious "enemies list." Still more sordid, at the height of the initial Whitewater investigation key Clinton aide Vincent Foster committed suicide under peculiar circum-

---

basing the level of contribution required of consumers on ability to pay.

Personal Responsibility: Under health reform, each individual and family should assume responsibility for protecting and promoting health and contributing to the cost of care. . . .

Effectiveness: The new system should deliver care, and innovation that works and that patients want. It should encourage the discovery of better treatments. It should make it possible for the academic community and health care providers to exercise effectively their responsibility to evaluate and improve health care by providing resources for the systematic study of health care outcomes.

Quality: The system should deliver high quality care and provide individuals with the information necessary to make informed health care choices.

Effective Management: By encouraging simplification and continuous improvement, as well as making the system easier to use for patients and providers, the health care system should focus on care, rather than administration. . . .

Local Responsibility: Working within the framework of national reform, the new health care system should allow states and local communities to design effective, high-quality systems of care that serve each of their citizens.

The White House Domestic Policy Council, *The President's Health Security Plan.* New York: Times Books, 1993.

---

stances, fueling lurid speculation that he had either been murdered or killed himself over imminent revelations about the administration's activities as well as those of the Clintons back in their days in Little Rock. Bill Clinton, meanwhile, had to dodge new accusations of sexual misconduct while governor, this time voiced by former Arkansas state employee Paula Jones, as well as later accusations that would arise that the White House had sold access to the president for campaign contributions.

All in all, the Clinton administration faced a steady shower of allegations, charges, revelations, explanations, and calls for investigations and special prosecutors. Yet Clinton remained as popular as ever as the economy continued to improve and America's sole superpower status remained secure. The public's lack of outrage at the president's various imbroglios surprised many, but the indifference had several explanations, including that the political depravity of Watergate and the epic sexual peccadilloes of John F. Kennedy had driven down Americans' expectations of presidential character. As Reagan had survived Iran-Contra, Clinton would probably survive the scandals that beset his tenure in the White House, although that remained unclear even halfway through his second term.

Indeed, Clinton would enjoy two major victories during his first administration: congressional approval of his budget, which included a substantial tax increase for the wealthy, and an expansion of the tax-credit system for low-income workers and the poor, among other radical changes from the Reagan-Bush approach. But Clinton's budget contained a good many spending cuts as well, which to some marked the Democratic president as a pragmatist—if not a conservative—willing to assume centrist positions to stay popular. Still, he also sponsored and pushed the Brady Bill through Congress, establishing a mandatory five-day waiting period for handgun purchases, a measure ardently opposed by conservatives in thrall to the powerful National Rifle Association.

If Clinton deserved credit for any single foreign policy

initiative in his first term, it would be for his administration's efforts to dismantle nuclear weapons' stockpiles along with the former Soviet Union, a process begun under President Bush. Clinton's foreign policy team considered the dismantling program as urgent as control of the Soviet tactical arsenal had become scattered among scores of local military commanders rather than centralized in Moscow, as had been the case during the Cold War. The administration's effort culminated in the U.S.-Russia-Ukraine Trilateral Statement and Annex, signed by the presidents of all three countries in Moscow on January 14, 1994, which led to the dismantling of all nuclear weapons in Ukraine. A psychological milestone was reached that same month when Clinton signed a landmark agreement with Boris Yeltsin to detarget U.S. and Russian strategic missiles: for the first time since the early 1950s no Russian missiles would be aimed at targets on U.S. soil. (Of course, the missiles still existed and could be retargeted in a matter of minutes.) Using nuclear disarmament, democracy building, and a joint belief in open markets as their common ground, Clinton and Yeltsin began to forge a fruitful relationship based on cautious trust. . . .

And no one could doubt that the Cold War was over once Yeltsin ordered the last Russian troops to evacuate the Baltic States and Germany.

By far the most serious foreign policy problem Clinton inherited, in addition to crises in North Korea, Haiti, and Somalia, was the Balkans. In 1992, the former Yugoslavia had disintegrated into battle zones over which three warring factions lay claim: Serbs (Eastern Orthodox), Croatians (Catholic), and Bosnians (Muslim). During the era of Communist leader Marshal Tito from 1946 to 1980, Yugoslavia had managed to harness its ethnic and religious animosities, but once the hatred was unleashed, the world was shocked by reports of ethnic cleansing, genocidal acts by Serb troops on Bosnia's civilians, and atrocities committed by Serbian forces against Bosnians held in detention camps.

Because the slaughter was covered extensively on television, the domestic political debate over what role Washington should play in ending the war threatened to become a foreign policy crisis for the Clinton administration. While congressional Republicans strongly favored providing arms to the Bosnian Muslims so they could better defend themselves against the Serbs, Clinton steadfastly supported the United Nations' ineffective peacekeeping efforts. While the United Nations made some progress—the sustained artillery shelling of Sarajevo's civilian population was sporadically halted and a war crimes tribunal established—the war continued. A turning point came on February 5, 1994, when sixty-eight civilians died in a mortar attack in Sarajevo. This time the Clinton administration called on NATO to protect the Bosnian Muslim "safe havens," and by April NATO jets were hitting Serb ground targets. Then a Bosnian-Croatian peace agreement was signed under U.S. prodding, ending the "war within a war" and suspending the second front. But a lasting ceasefire proved elusive. Clinton found himself buffeted between the need to maintain NATO and U.N. credibility and an unwillingness to commit U.S. troops.

After months of a temporary cease-fire, Clinton called for a peace summit to be held at Wright-Patterson Air Force Base in Dayton, Ohio, far from war-ravaged Bosnia. With Slobodan Milosevic representing the Bosnian Serbs, Alija Izetbegovic serving as the voice of the Bosnian government, and Franjo Tudjman standing in for the Bosnian Croatians, a tenacious U.S. mediating team brokered a peaceful settlement that solved territorial differences and constitutional questions while forcing everybody involved to lay down their arms. The tenets of the agreement reached at Dayton on November 21, 1995, were officially memorialized in the Paris Peace Accord signed December 14 by the presidents of Bosnia, Serbia, and Croatia. That same month Clinton, despite staunch opposition, committed American troops to Bosnia as part of a NATO-led multinational force deployed to prevent further bloodshed and to support the new peace agreement. Sending in the U.S. troops, Clinton told the nation in a televised address, would signal that America was not shirking its responsibilities as the world's most powerful nation. Clinton went forward with the deployment, and 20,000 U.S. troops joined 40,000 from other NATO and Partnership for Peace countries. The U.S. Congress never officially supported the president's decision to deploy U.S. troops, but did not try to block it. From the start the NATO Implementation Force did an exceptional job of maintaining the cease-fire, stopping the widespread killing of civilians and restoring security to Sarajevo, where people could once again walk the streets in safety. "We stood for peace in Bosnia," Clinton proclaimed in his January 23, 1996, State of the Union address. "Remember the skeletal prisoners, the mass graves, the campaign to rape and torture, the endless lines of refugees, the threat of a spreading war. All these threats, all these horrors have now begun to give way to a promise of peace."

Clinton's move to the right in both international and domestic affairs was caused in part by the Republicans' considerable victories in the 1994 midterm elections, which put the GOP back in control of both houses of Congress—a clear indication that for all his popularity, the president had no party coattails at all. For the next year the most compelling figure in U.S. politics was the new Republican Speaker of the House, Newt Gingrich, a forceful and bumptious Georgia conservative intent on transferring power from the federal government to the states by cutting both taxes and spending in what he called the "Contract with America." The Speaker came across as a true Reaganite, and the conservatives who flocked to his cause began to talk of his challenging Clinton in 1996. But then Gingrich misstepped, signing a lucrative book contract that seemed ethically questionably to some, after which his Democratic opponents took aim at his every move. The partisan rancor rose, and when Clinton and the Republican-led Congress were unable to agree on a federal budget the government was forced to shut down, first in November 1995 and again in December lasting until January 1996, to substantial hue and cry if with little effect on the workings of the nation. Still, the public blamed Congress for the impasse, and the ineptitude of Gingrich's responses to it sent his popularity ratings plummeting. By mid-1996 Clinton had recouped his losses and benefited from the Republicans' disarray to increase his standing with the American people.

Among the most significant reasons for Clinton's resurgence was that he had once again shown a remarkable facility for co-opting the most popular parts of the Republican program as his own, including the political hot potato of welfare reform. After the 1994 congressional elections put the GOP back in charge of the legislature, Clinton came out in favor of a program that would transfer much of the welfare system from the federal government to the states. The plan would also put a five-year limit on welfare benefits to any family, require adults receiving welfare to go to work after two years, and deny assistance to noncitizens. With this President Clinton not only helped bring an end to federal welfare programs that had been in place since the [1930s] but also rejected an important symbol of what had been the Democratic Party's long-term commitment to the poor. To mitigate this apparent coldheartedness the president approved a ninety-cent increase in the minimum wage and accepted a measure enabling Americans to continue their employer-sponsored health insurance when they changed jobs. Such gestures to the left were not enough, and overall Clinton's ongoing move to the political right alienated the liberal wing of his party and all but ensured a challenge to Vice President Gore for the Democratic presidential nomination in 2000.

In 1996, however, that economic focus was most of the reason Clinton and Gore had no difficulty winning their party's renomination. . . . Meanwhile a large field of Republican hopefuls duked it out through the primaries, from which Senate Majority Leader Bob Dole of Kansas emerged with the nomination, in part because he had allowed his natural sense of humor to show through his erstwhile image for meanness. Dole selected as his running mate enthusiastic, conservative former New York congressman, Reagan Cabinet member, and Buffalo Bills quarterback Jack Kemp. Once again, third-party nuisance H. Ross Perot complicated the race and took 7.9 million votes, while Clinton won with 45.6 million popular and 379 electoral-college votes to Dole's tallies of 37.8 million and 159.

Unlike his first term, Clinton's second administration began with international matters on the front burner, where President Bush's old nemesis Saddam Hussein had put them early in 1997 by trying to block U.N. representatives from inspecting Iraq's weapons installations, as had been agreed at the end of the Persian Gulf War. Clinton had no intention of putting up with such intransigence from the world's most troublesome dictator and started assembling a multinational coalition should the need arise to take military action in the region. This proved more difficult than it had been for Bush, as in the absence of an Iraqi attack the Arab states saw little reason to join an alliance against Saddam. Clinton spent much of his second term combating international terrorism and made goodwill trips to South Africa, Russia, and Northern Ireland.

Clinton was happy to immerse himself in foreign affairs, particularly when in early 1998 he was accused of having had sexual relations with a twenty-one-year-old White House intern and then encouraging her to lie about it to a federal grand jury. This debilitating new scandal drove the Mideast and virtually everything else from the front pages of America's newspapers, but the economy continued to perform well and polls showed that Clinton remained popular even after he was forced to make a televised address to the nation on August 17 admitting that he had indeed had an "inappropriate" relationship with Monica Lewinsky. On September 11, 1998, Independent Counsel Kenneth Starr's scathing report charged Clinton with eleven counts of impeachable offenses that ranged from obstruction of justice to perjury. It looked as if the remainder of Clinton's second term would be an extremely turbulent one.

Clinton Survives Impeachment

Kenneth T. Walsh

On August 5, 1994, an independent counsel headed by Kenneth Starr was impaneled to investigate Bill and Hillary Clinton's 1982 Whitewater land deal. The investigation eventually revealed that Clinton had had a sexual affair with White House intern Monica Lewinsky during 1995 and 1996 and had lied about it before a grand jury. This resulted in the House of Representatives voting to impeach Clinton in October 1998. In poll after poll, however, two-thirds of the American public stood against Clinton's impeachment, and the Senate did not have the two-thirds majority vote necessary to remove him from office. In this selection Kenneth T. Walsh, a journalist for *U.S. News & World Report*, gives an overview of the impeachment of Bill Clinton.

The finale, when it came at last, generated no joy or anger, only relief. After 13 months during which the plot veered madly from the titillating to the arcane, from tragedy to farce, when some of the nation's best lawyers haggled over what "is" is, the long-awaited denouement seemed devoid of exalted purpose or the sense that historic principle was at stake. Instead, the Senate's acquittal of William Jefferson Clinton in his impeachment trial seemed more like the last gasp of an implausible soap opera than the conclusion of a constitutional crisis.

The outcome had been expected; the only surprise was

Excerpted from "The Price of Victory," by Kenneth T. Walsh, *U.S. News & World Report*, February 22, 1999. Copyright ©1999 by U.S. News & World Report. Visit www.usnews.com for additional information.

the weakness of the support for conviction. The Senate declared President Clinton not guilty of perjury by a 55-to-45 vote and acquitted him of obstruction of justice by an aptly muddled 50-50—well short of the two-thirds majority, or 67 votes, required to remove him from office. Afterward, he played his concluding scene as a model of conciliation in a brief statement of apology. As he moved to leave the Rose Garden, a reporter asked whether it was time to forgive and forget. Clinton stopped in his tracks, paused, and turned again to the cameras. "I believe any person who asks for forgiveness has to be prepared to give it," the president said with a bittersweet smile.

Americans Tuned Out

It remains to be seen whether Washington's tribes, and the president himself, will really make peace or renew hostilities. The epilogue on impeachment is still to be written as the Senate decides in the next few weeks whether to censure Clinton for his misconduct. But most Americans tuned out the impeachment drama long ago. Part of the reason may be that the country cannot yet fully assess what—if anything—all the *sturm und drang* has meant. "This is a little like Vietnam," says David Blankenhorn, president of the Institute for American Values. "The war ended in 1973, but we fought over its meaning for a long time after that. The impeachment conflict is ending, but I think we will be discussing what it means for quite some time. This has been a traumatic experience."

Perhaps. But early indications are that the public was so turned off by the long-running Washington melodrama that it would sooner forget the case than mull its true meaning. In a *U.S. News* poll, respondents said they were "disgusted" by the scandal. Everything about it: the players, the politics, the partisanship, the policy put on hold while the scandal ground on. And, contrary to the pop punditry, those surveyed said they didn't believe there would be a lasting scar, that the nation's moral fiber would fray, or that it would spawn a generation of liars.

Other than reaffirming that the constitutional system

seems to work just fine, in grand historical terms the past 13 months may not mean much else. Yet in a messy way, the spectacle has much to say about America's fundamental values and politics as it approaches the millennium.

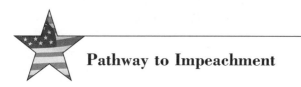 **Pathway to Impeachment**

Bill Clinton's impeachment culminated in February 1999 when the Senate failed to muster the votes to remove him from office. But the long road to impeachment began in January 1994 when Attorney General Janet Reno appointed an independent counsel to investigate Clinton's 1982 Whitewater land deal. The Los Angeles Times *published a timeline that detailed Clinton's troubles from 1994 to 1999.*

1994

January: Independent counsel is formed to investigate Whitewater land deal.

May 6: Paula Corbin Jones files suit alleging Clinton sexually harassed her.

1995

July: White House employee Monica S. Lewinsky and Bill Clinton have an affair.

1996

Nov. 5: Clinton is reelected with 49% of the vote.

1997

May 24: Clinton ends his affair with Lewinsky.

September: White House employee Linda Tripp begins recording her telephone conversations with Lewinsky.

Nov. 24: Tripp is subpoenaed in the Jones case.

Dec. 19: Lewinsky is subpoenaed in the Jones case.

Dec. 26: Lewinsky leaves her new job at the Pentagon.

1998

Jan. 7: Lewinsky signs affidavit in the Jones case saying she had no sexual relationship with Clinton.

Jan. 12: Tripp provides Starr's office with taped conversations between herself and Lewinsky.

Jan. 13: Tripp, wearing a hidden microphone for the FBI, meets with

This psychodrama showed the extent to which the presidency, which for a half century was seen as a heroic institution that embodied the nation's dreams, aspirations, ethics, and sense of dignity, has been miniaturized. It has,

---

Lewinsky for lunch.

Jan. 26: Clinton, in a deposition to lawyers for Jones, denies a sexual relationship with Lewinsky; Clinton publicly declares: "I did not have sexual relations with that woman. . . . I never told anybody to lie."

Jan. 27: Starr opens grand jury inquiry into Lewinsky matter.

April 1: Jones suit is dismissed by Arkansas federal Judge Susan Webber Wright, whose decision states that the charges do not meet the definition of sexual harassment. Clinton, traveling in Africa, reacts gleefully.

April 15: Jones decides to appeal the order dismissing her lawsuit.

June 30: Tripp testifies to Starr's grand jury.

July 28: Starr grants Lewinsky immunity from prosecution if she will testify truthfully to the grand jury.

Aug. 3: Clinton gives a DNA sample to Starr's investigators that is later found to match a stain on one of Lewinsky's dresses.

Aug. 6: Lewinsky testifies to the grand jury.

Aug. 17: Clinton, after questioning by the grand jury, acknowledges in a televised speech that he had "inappropriate intimate contact"with Lewinsky.

Sept. 11: Congress releases the Starr report.

Oct. 8: House votes 258–176 to authorize Judiciary Committee to conduct a broad impeachment inquiry.

Nov. 13: Clinton, without apologizing or admitting guilt, agrees to pay Jones $850,000 to forgo appealing her sexual harassment lawsuit.

Dec. 11–12: House Judiciary Committee approves four articles of impeachment.

Dec. 19: The full House approves two of the articles of impeachment, charging Clinton with lying in his grand jury testimony and obstructing justice by covering up his affair with Lewinsky.

1999

Jan. 7: Impeachment trial opens in the Senate as senators are sworn in as jurors.

Jan. 14: House Republicans, acting as Clinton's prosecutors, present evidence to Senate.

Los Angeles Times, "Pathway to Peril," January 31, 1999.

---

in fact, become a cog in an all-pervasive celebrity culture that raises notoriety to a value unto itself, whether it is born of achievement, humiliation, character, or stupidity. At the center of it all is President Clinton, who over six years has become the most ubiquitous figure not only in American politics but in American culture. For the past year, the nation has been forced to live in Bill's Universe, a combination of *Melrose Place, Law and Order,* and *Entertainment Tonight.* Amazingly, the president of the United States has become a front-page favorite of the trashiest and trendiest tabloids, a spot once reserved only for the hottest rockers and film stars. "It's a jarring note," says a senior White House official. "It doesn't matter if it's fame or infamy; if you're on TV, you're 'in,' whether you're Charlie Sheen or Latrell Sprewell or the pope."

This is not a culture in which Clinton is uncomfortable. In fact, America's greatest TV president helped create it. "Playing the saxophone, talking about [his] underwear, Bill Clinton has shown that he is a creature of the celebrity culture," says New York University sociologist Todd Gitlin. "The distinction between public and private life is lost on him." Adds a Clinton friend: "This president viscerally prefers intimacy to distance, and that has both positive and negative consequences. It means he scores high on any measure of whether 'he cares about me'—but intimacy also is the enemy of dignity." Those who ask whether this episode establishes important precedents might want to consider whether we'll soon have another president like Clinton.

The core of the problem remains Clinton's flawed character. His legendary self-indulgence led him to conduct a reckless affair at the White House with former intern Monica Lewinsky over a period of 18 months. Perhaps the most remarkable finding of a new *U.S. News* poll is that Clinton is now considered to have the worst moral standards of any modern president. Fifty-six percent of voters rated him at the bottom. And in a note that must be particularly galling to Clinton, his rating was far worse than that of Richard Nixon, the president who resigned rather than face impeachment and a man whom Clinton has always reviled. Nixon came in a distant second on the immorality index with 14 percent.

Still, Clinton's job approval has remained consistent over the past year, according to the *U.S. News* poll conducted by Republican Ed Goeas and Democrat Celinda Lake: Fifty-eight percent of voters endorsed his job performance in January 1998; and 57 percent approve today. Most of the disparity between voters' judgment of his character and of his job performance is due, quite simply, to the booming economy. The poll finds that 73 percent of voters feel that because the economy is in such good shape, people will look the other way as long as Clinton is reprimanded for his misconduct. "They're not setting the moral or character issues aside," says former White House press secretary Mike McCurry, "but they see them as one factor that can be outweighed by other factors. People make that calibration, and they'll do that for every other public official from now on."

At least for today, the president seems to be a national CEO and little more. Republican Sen. Charles Grassley of Iowa says it will take 10 years to build up the presidency's "moral authority" again.

Virtually Everything Was Revealed

It was a year in which Independent Counsel Kenneth Starr pushed Monica Lewinsky's mom to tears, forced Secret Service agents to tell all, pried into bookstore purchases, pumped Lewinsky's therapist for information. When virtually everything was revealed: thong underwear, cigars as sex toys, the president's semen on the former intern's blue dress. When Lewinsky's private conversations were tape-recorded by her then friend, Linda Tripp, and played for the world; when the Starr report, in all its graphic detail, was published on the Internet; when the president's depositions and his grand jury testimony were televised. It was a year of outrageous outings: Rep. Dan Burton admitting an out-of-wedlock child; Reps. Helen Chenoweth and

Henry Hyde and then incoming House Speaker Bob Livingston admitting affairs.

"There has been a collapse of any distinction between public and private, and that is a serious threat to our society, not just our politics," says Blankenhorn of the Institute for American Values. "Privacy isn't just a luxury. Privacy is necessary to human flourishing."

No Turning Back

Certainly, privacy had been in trouble for years in America's confessional culture, where people brawl on television

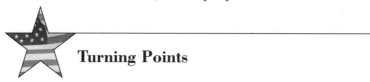

Turning Points

In the chronology of events leading up to President Clinton's impeachment and trial, a handful of moments proved to be pivotal. In many cases, the consequences were not apparent at the time.

November 1995: With the federal government closed by a political budget showdown, White House intern Monica S. Lewinsky delivers pizza to the Oval Office. She and Clinton begin a clandestine affair.

Lewinsky normally wouldn't have had an easy time getting in the president's office, but the government shutdown meant most White House staff had the day off.

May 1997: The Supreme Court allows Paula Corbin Jones' sexual harassment lawsuit against Clinton to proceed.

The decision was 9–0. But justices may now wonder whether they were right to predict that the case would have little impact on the presidency.

September 1997: Negotiations to settle the Jones lawsuit collapse.

Clinton's lawyers were ready to settle for $700,000. But Jones' husband wanted an apology from the president, and First Lady Hillary Rodham Clinton objected to that.

after revealing embarrassing intimacies and where callers phone talk-show hosts to reveal their most intimate problems. But the Clinton-Lewinsky saga dealt privacy another devastating blow. "The public probing of sexual behavior has made the mainstream press and the highest institutions of our government into nothing but an episode of *Jerry Springer*," says David Harris, a law and ethics professor at the University of Toledo.

Perhaps there can be no turning back. "At this stage, there is no possibility of re-creating a kind of safe harbor of personal privacy," says James Davison Hunter, a sociologist

---

January 1998: Atty. Gen. Janet Reno approves a request from independent counsel Kenneth W. Starr to investigate the Lewinsky matter.

Reno could have assigned the issue to Justice Department lawyers or sought the appointment of another independent counsel. But Starr aides told her they could intercept a crime as it was being committed.

February 1998: Clinton rejects his lawyers' suggestion that he correct his deposition in the Jones lawsuit.

Witnesses have 30 days to correct errors in testimony. Clinton would have taken legal and political risks in clarifying his deposition, but he could have weakened the charges against him.

August 1998: Clinton stumbles in his grand jury testimony, insisting he never touched Lewinsky sexually.

The president intended to stick to a carefully drafted statement on his contact with Lewinsky. But under questioning he went further, giving Starr's prosecutors more evidence.

November 1998: Buoyed by victory in congressional elections, Democrats fail to press for a quick censure resolution.

Some now think they might have headed off impeachment if they had pushed for peace instead of prematurely declaring victory. Others contend it was already too late.

Los Angeles Times, "Pathway to Peril," January 31, 1999.

---

at the University of Virginia. "From this point on, conservatives and progressives, Democrats and Republicans, will view private life as fair game in ways that I think neither side will be happy with and certainly not comfortable with."

Yet the Clinton scandal did at least seem to sensitize everyday people to questions about society's loss of privacy. Boston University sociologist Alan Wolfe says that while most middle-class suburbanites disdain an "everything goes" attitude, they are also "reluctant to pass judgment on how other people act and think." While they have concerns about family breakdown, they are reluctant to turn the clock back on the sexual revolution and return to more traditional values. "With the president they were even more understanding and nuanced than I would have thought," Wolfe says. "They concluded that adultery and lying are inseparable. To forgive one is to forgive the other."

Americans also were offended by the overreaching Starr investigation, realizing for the first time prosecutors' tremendous power. But this may result not in any cultural shift toward preservation of privacy but in a simple backlash against the independent-counsel law, which expired June 30, 1999. If the law is renewed by Congress, it very likely will be scaled back dramatically to curb the nearly unlimited legal authority of such prosecutors.

Sparkle Has Left His Eyes

Friends say [Clinton] is concerned about being marginalized now that attention will inevitably focus on choosing his successor. Democratic strategists admit that the impeachment struggle may have inflated Clinton's job-approval ratings by about 10 points; one theory among his allies is that voters gave him an artificial boost to send a message that they didn't want him removed. Now that the threat is over, some Democrats fear that Clinton's job approval will fade, weakening his position.

Pals who saw him recently were struck by how the sparkle had left his eyes and how weary he seemed. Asked how he was doing, he said, "We've had a good day," as if he were not thinking too far ahead. Yet there are other signs that, with the impeachment trial finally over, his old resilience is returning. He told aides recently that he wanted them to continue generating initiatives until the very end of his administration. In fact, he said, "I want to have a new policy proposal on my last day in office so my successor can work on it."

But there have been more hostile conversations as well. Despite his public posture of conciliation, Clinton has been talking with confidants about what one calls "rolling heads" in 2000—defeating at least some of the House prosecutors and vulnerable Republicans who voted to impeach him.

All this ensures more unexpected twists yet to be played out in the psychodrama known as the Clinton presidency.

Perot's Reform Party Continues Its Success

Steven E. Schier

During the spring and summer of 1992 the presidential campaign became a three-way race. Texas billionaire Ross Perot, who had made a fortune in computer programming, ran as an independent candidate under the banner of his recently created Reform Party. Perot developed a strong following, and by April 1992 his popularity had climbed to 30 percent in the opinion polls. By July he was running ahead of Clinton. After running an erratic race, the Texas businessman received about 19 percent of the total votes in November—the best showing of a third-party candidate in seventy years. When Perot ran again in the 1996 election, Americans did not seem as enamored of him and he received only 9 percent of the votes cast.

In this selection Steven E. Schier, the chair of the political science department at Carleton College in Northfield, Minnesota, and a political analyst for WCCO television in Minneapolis, writes that the Reform Party did not die when Perot failed to be elected president. It was once again thrust into the headlines in 1998 when former bodybuilder and wrestling star Jesse "the Body" Ventura won the Minnesota governor race under the Reform Party banner. By defeating two well-known mainstream candidates who had the major financial backing of their parties, Ventura shook up the political establishment in the liberal state. Schier contends that Ventura's election proved that many voters were sick and tired of politics as usual and would even vote for an inexperienced candidate who was forthright and honest with his opinions—and who put on a good show on television. Although Ventura's victory was particular to Minnesota, Schier believes that the trends expressed by the candidate and the voters could well be applied to most states across the country.

In the wake of his stunning election as Minnesota's next governor, former World Wrestling Federation superstar Jesse Ventura presides as a genuine cultural phenomenon. The darling of the media, particularly televised "infotainment" programs, he allowed over one hundred desperate reporters to interview him during his stopover at the National Governors' Conference shortly after his victory. He has published a book, for which he was paid in the mid six figures, with a major publishing house. Stores in Minnesota feature T-shirts proclaiming "My Governor Can Kick Your Governor's Ass" and, more tamely, "My Governor Can Beat Up Your Governor." Jesse—that's what infatuated Minnesotans call their new governor—loves the media, thinks fast on his feet, and presents himself with a testosterone-juiced air of authority. Americans will see a lot of him over the next four years.

If all this seems a funny political sideshow, it isn't. Ventura's election carries important implications for politics in Minnesota and the nation as a whole. His triumph seems so beyond the pale that a lot must be happening in our politics to cause it. And a lot is. Jesse's ascendancy underscores the great and growing weaknesses of [the Democratic and Republican] parties with the public. It reveals that third parties have a future in American politics only if national campaign finance and voter registration rules come to resemble those now in force in Minnesota. The success of

Ventura's unorthodox, low-budget campaign ads exposes the shortcomings of conventional political advertising. And, perhaps most disturbingly, Jesse's rise to the top confirms the growing power of celebrity and entertainment in American politics.

Major Parties in Disrepute

Jesse's victory required a harmonic convergence of legal and political circumstances that took Minnesota's quirky political populism to a new level. During the '90s, voters in Minnesota have taken a liking to candidates who attack the "political establishment" of the state from all manner of directions. In 1990 and 1996, [Senator] Paul Wellstone's tie-dyed leftist insurgency carried him to victory over establishment Republican Rudy Boschwitz. Rod Grams, as emphatically to the right as Wellstone is to the left, won a Senate seat during the 1994 nationwide Republican insurgency, defeating Ann Wynia, a conventional liberal well-known and widely respected among Minnesota's political establishment. Arne Carlson, the outgoing Republican governor, is a scrapper who has been at war with the activists in his own party for years, and has won office twice despite being denied endorsement for the party primary by two consecutive state Republican conventions. Jesse is the culmination of this trend, rocking the political establishment from the "radical" center.

Why do Minnesotans like the insurgent style in their statewide candidates? The answer lies in the decay of the two major parties in the state. Two decades ago, scholars routinely ranked Minnesota as a state with a strong party system. No more. Though both the Democratic and Republican parties of the state still boast big budgets and many office-holders, they have lost their hold over the voters.

Over the last 20 years, attendance at the precinct caucuses has dwindled to the point where the total number of those showing up for both parties' caucuses wouldn't even fill the 50,000 seats of the Metrodome (home of the Twins and Vikings). Party activists have become extreme, standing well to the left and right of most raters. In addition, established interest groups—the AFL-CIO and Education Minnesota (the modestly titled state teachers' union) among the Democrats, and anti-tax and Christian conservatives among the Republicans—set the platform agenda and often hand-pick the endorsed candidates. The result is that each party's endorsing convention has become an outpost of exotic politics. Evangelical religion is heavy in the air when Republicans meet, and this year Democrats passed a rule declaring their convention must be "fragrance free" lest any delegate's perfume offend another's allergies. The result of this trend? The public says no, thank you, to endorsed candidates. . . .

Well Known from His Wrestling Days

With the parties now in disrepute, Minnesota's elections have become more candidate-centered, particularly at the statewide level, where television rules. Those endorsed candidates who have won statewide all had an insurgent quality that blurred any association they had with the activists and interest groups of their political party. Each winner got around the unpopularity of their party via personal style. And in this lay Jesse Ventura's great opportunity—style.

Ventura, a Minneapolis native, was well known from his wrestling days. In recent years, he had reigned as a local talk radio host, where he spouted a vague constellation of views. Though he knew little about the actual operations of government, he claimed to be socially libertarian regarding abortion and gay rights, yet a strong fiscal conservative. As Mayor of the Minneapolis suburb of Brooklyn Park in the early '90s, he feuded frequently with the city council. His record in office was mixed; crime went down but taxes went up.

When Ventura announced his candidacy, his slogan was "Retaliate in '98," a sort of "up yours" to the Minnesota political establishment. The state legislature's handling of the huge $2 billion budget surplus in 1998 was the catalyst for Ventura's candidacy. The legislature returned less than half of it in tax relief, saving some as a fiscal reserve and using the rest for a variety of spending programs. Ventura promised to return the entire surplus if he were elected.

Through September, most observers viewed Ventura as an amusing sideshow. The victors in the party primaries, Democratic Attorney General Hubert "Skip" Humphrey (son of the famous Hubert) and Republican St. Paul Mayor Norm Coleman, are both life-long government employees and officeholders. Each was personally cautious and "button-down" in demeanor. They provided a nice gray background for Jesse's campaign antics. Every act needs a straight man, and Jesse had two of them. The great mistake during the fall came from the [Democratic candidate]. Hopeful that Ventura would draw "angry white male" voters away from [the Republican], Humphrey insisted that Ventura be included in each of 10 debates. Jesse had his stage. In the debates, he stated his views in a blustery, candid, and disarming fashion. For instance, when asked whether he favored state aid for college students, Jesse disapproved and called on students to "get a job!" It became clear that he knew little about policy, but he did speak sincerely and displayed a commanding, charismatic presence.

Coleman and Humphrey largely ignored Jesse and sniped at each other during the debates, allowing Jesse to seem appealingly anti-political. . . .

[Ventura] was able to hire populist image-meister Bill Hillsman, a Twin Cities advertising executive who was the inspiration behind the successful and unorthodox ads that propelled underdog [Senator Paul] Wellstone into the Senate in 1990. Hillsman's ads, particularly one featuring the Jesse Ventura "action figure" fighting a corrupt lobbyist "action figure," proved effective and memorable. Without the ads, Ventura could not have eked out his 55,000 vote plurality. . . .

Ventura was also helped by the fact that Minnesota is one of only seven states that allow voters to register on election day. A surge of young, first-time voters took advantage of last-minute registration to cast their ballots for

Jesse. Minnesota's turnout led the nation as 60.1 percent of those eligible went to the polls. Statewide, a remarkable one in six voters registered on election day, the highest proportion of the electorate to do so since the mid-'70s when the law was first implemented. . . .

Sharing a Common Disgust

Some reasons for Jesse's triumph are specific to Minnesota, but many are not. Our national parties share many of the weaknesses of their Minnesota counterparts. . . .

The Ventura candidacy is a warning bell to the national parties about their extremism and dependence on powerful interest groups. For evidence on both counts, one need look no further than the U.S. House of Representatives. There, the caucuses of both parties are dominated by ideologues of the left and right, each well-supported by the contributions of their favorite organized interests. Ventura's victory suggests that time may be running out on such conventional politics. The Minnesota public shares a common disgust of it with the national public, and happened to find an outlet for this discontent in Ventura.

The success of Hillsman's ads for Ventura illustrates another weakness in national electoral politics. Political consultants, including those who worked for Coleman and Humphrey, rely on shopworn advertising styles during campaigns, often featuring heavily negative messages. Indeed, ads in one state often seem virtually indistinguishable from ads shown in every other. Why is this? According to Hillsman, it all goes back to the desire of consultants to make a buck. Since ad consultants are paid in a percentage of the overall ad "buy," the incentive is for quick work and heavy quantity in campaign advertising. Big buys mean big bucks for consultants. Since certain ads have worked in the past, qualitative experimentation of the sort done by Hillsman is risky. Further, quality ads can prove effective at a small fraction of the cost of conventional ads, as did Hillsman's, and what consultant wants to slice his/her income drastically? Hillsman argues that spending limits might actually improve campaign ads by shifting the focus from quantity to quality.

The Need for Campaign Finance Reform

A third lesson for national politics from Minnesota is that third parties have no chance in national elections without campaign finance reform. True, Perot did break through at the presidential level, but only by spending tens of millions of his own dollars first. That's a high cost of entry. If the threshold is high at the presidential level, it is virtually insurmountable in congressional elections, where no public financing exists. Unless third parties can earn public matching funds, they will be spent to death by the two major parties, regardless of how attractive any third party candidate proves to be. The current campaign finance laws allow the activist zealots and powerful interests dominating our two major parties to maintain their grip on the electorate. To loosen that grip, the laws must change.

A final and disturbing lesson from Minnesota concerns the triumph of style over substance. True, Jesse Ventura placed himself somewhere between Humphrey's liberalism and Coleman's conservatism, but it was never very clear just where he stood. Some of his ideas voiced during the campaign—such as prohibiting welfare recipients from having cable television and requiring the cable companies to enforce this law—are just plain wacky. Now that Ventura's elected, he has stopped calling for a refund of last year's surplus to taxpayers. Minnesotans are waiting for their [governor] to figure out his positions on major issues. A tax cut? Spending increases? Spending cuts? Education reforms? Who knows? Jesse is very much a work in progress.

If elections worked the way they are supposed to, Minnesotans would have known the answers to these questions before the election. Certainly, Humphrey and Coleman showered them with policy detail. That didn't matter to many voters, including the 46 percent of those under the age of 30 who gave Ventura their vote. Jesse provided a little information about the issues—and a lot of entertainment. It was fun. It just wasn't substantive.

The generational aspect of Ventura's victory is ultimately the most disturbing. Younger voters like Jesse's act, and hate the language of conventional politics. A lot of standard political discourse is pretty tacky, but at its core, it is more substantive than anything Jesse has yet uttered. As infotainment becomes the rage on local news, Americans may come to demand more infotainment candidates like Jesse. He's fun, he's a celebrity and he's unconventional. Can he govern? Who knows?

CHAPTER 2

War and Peace
After the Cold War

AMERICA'S DECADES

Eastern Europe Awakens to Freedom

Mort Rosenblum

As the 1990s dawned, Eastern Europe awakened from the forty-five-year-long Communist nightmare. The entire post–World War II generation in Poland, Czechoslovakia, Hungary, Romania, and other Eastern Bloc countries had grown up in a totalitarian society where speaking one's mind could mean the loss of a job, a prison sentence, or even death. When the Soviet Union collapsed and Eastern European countries held democratic elections for the first time, it was overwhelmingly emotional for citizens who dared not even speak the word *democracy* for almost five decades.

Mort Rosenblum was among the first Western journalists to arrive in Romania after the fall of dictator Nicolae Ceausescu. He received the 1990 Overseas Press Club Hal Boyle Award for International Reporting for his coverage of the Eastern European revolution. In addition, he was the editor in chief of the *International Herald Tribune* and the author of several books.

Czechoslovaks jingled their keys in the air, and forty-one years of Communist Party totalitarianism fell away before their eyes. East Germans awoke one morning to find their hated wall had crumbled beneath its own weight. Ro-

Excerpted from *Moments of Revolution: Eastern Europe,* by Mort Rosenblum (New York: Stewart, Tabori, & Chang, 1990). Copyright ©1990 by Mort Rosenblum. Reprinted with permission from the Carol Mann Agency.

manians fought a bitter war against terror in their streets, but it was over in a week. From the Baltic to the Balkans, in a matter of months, the earth shifted. The words *freedom* and *democracy* were repeated again and again. But this was not about words.

Zdenek Machon was among a quarter-million Czechoslovaks who, on a December Sunday too cold for standing still, came back one more time to [Prague's] Wenceslas Square. He stood in a vast sea of arms outstretched in victory. Like the others, he made a triumphant V with his fingers. But he could not quite manage the national anthem. His voice cracked and boiled over from the heat of revolution.

"I can look people directly in the eye now, people from other countries," he told an American reporter, who was nearly as overcome as Machon. "We are a free people again. We are part of Europe again." A big man with a thick mustache, he showed no embarrassment at the tears trickling down his face. It was the students who first rose up, and Machon has three in his family. "I am so thankful to my children for setting us free," he said. "And I am so happy that they can now live their lives in freedom."

The crowd was listening to [President] Vaclav Havel, speaking from a balcony over the lovely wide boulevard of art nouveau elegance that, in a past era, was a spiritual heart of Europe. Havel, jailed, muzzled, reviled [under communism], had hammered away at his theme: the communist state was immoral, illogical, and inhuman. Though Czechoslovakia's best-known playwright, no one at home had seen his work on stage since Soviet tanks silenced the Prague [Revolt during] Spring of 1968. But, in the end, Havel brought down the house.

Machon tried to describe what he felt. He heard the words coming out—freedom and democracy—and they did not satisfy him. As a geophysicist, he explained, he traveled to conferences in the West and found himself feeling half a man. He knew what his nation was and what someday it could be again. This was that day. "It is a wonderful day, wonderful," he said. "How can I say it?" Instead of trying further, he hugged the reporter and wept again.

Iron Curtain Rusted Away

That was revolution in Eastern Europe. There were the grand themes. An iron curtain rusted and flaked away. A political order was overturned, and an economic system collapsed. Nikita Khrushchev's [1960s] shoe-banging on a table at the United Nations was a muffled echo in the past. But for all the sweeping ideology, the cold war clichés, the terrifying and tender symbols, this was a close-up revolution. It was the sum of personal victories. After four decades people found their dignity and reaffirmed their values. This was a triumph of human spirit.

Power came from faceless crowds, the huge masses that finally were too big to bully. But each individual in every crowd knew what was at risk: a job, the few privileges wheedled from the system—or a life. Beyond the noise of chants and gunfire, there was a lilting [melodic passage]. Hummed, strummed, sung out loud in a half-dozen languages, it was the same haunting melody of the American civil rights era, "We Shall Overcome."

In groups, individuals overcame, and they found again a national pride that was smothered by two generations of outside occupation.

Havel spoke not only for his own people in his presidential message on New Year's Day, 1990: "Everywhere in the world, people were surprised how these malleable, humiliated, cynical citizens of Czechoslovakia, who seemingly believed in nothing, found the tremendous strength within a few weeks to cast off the totalitarian system, in an entirely peaceful and dignified manner."

Havel raised two crucial questions: "Where did young people who had never known another system get their longing for truth, their love of freedom, their political imagination, their civic courage and civic responsibility? How did their parents, precisely the generation thought to have been lost, join them?"

Starting a New Life

In the heat of a revolution in Romania that was dignified if not peaceful, those same questions arose. On that Friday, December 22, when [Communist dictator] Nicolae Ceausescu fell, die-hard Securitate commandos tried to seize the television station. After midnight shells slammed into the thirteen-story building, and bullets shattered its windows. Marin Constantin, a producer of children's programs, took charge of the eighth floor. He doused the lights. When an overhead fixture would not turn off, he deftly smashed it with a chair. Gratiela Ripeanu and Elena Maria Ionescu, writers whose job had been cheerleading for Ceausescu, gaily shepherded visitors and colleagues to cover.

Throughout a terrifying siege, the little band joked about their plight while they privately exulted at their triumph. As dawn approached, they taught several foreign reporters an anthem from a past moment of glory, a song not heard in public since their parents were children: "Awake, Romania, from the mortal sleep into which you have been lulled by the evil tyrants."

For the next week, in the rubble of Bucharest, awakened Romanians seized passing journalists by the arm. Toma Cornelia seized mine. "You tell the world that we are not what people think we are," he said. "You tell them what we have done here." He had a sister who had moved to Loveland, Colorado. She could take no more of Nicolae Ceausescu. "You tell her we are starting a new life," Cornelia said. "Tell her we are waiting for her."

But he had the look I had just seen on the face of Zdenek Machon in Prague. It was a look that reporters came to recognize in all the revolutions, the tormented tableau of pride and pain fighting for the same space. Beneath joy and fervor, there was a chill of fear. Hardly anyone had any illusions about the future. Big Brother was going, but he was leaving a hell of a mess behind. And in case the repentant family missed him, he was not far away.

The notion of struggle, so beloved to Marxist-Leninists, was about to become hard reality. Struggling was what one was supposed to do against capitalists and imperialists who put self above society. In real life, people knew their enemy as an alien apparatus called the state. But in a system freed of choice, they endured or eluded. Some risked and suffered. Against a seamless monolith, however, few struggled. Lines were long, but there were basic necessities at the end. If not many thrived, no one starved. It was an old bargain: people pretended to work; the state pretended to pay them. Life went on without the intrusion of election campaigns or storms in the stock market.

Brink of Economic Ruin

Revolutions brought back the possibility to choose, but East Europeans made few choices. As one analyst put it, they had broken the eggs but still had to make the omelette. Interim governments scheduled elections for people whose democratic traditions had been stifled since the 1930s. Economists shaped a free market for societies without capital or credit. Anything was possible, including calamity.

Poland was as much a source of concern as of inspiration. The Solidarity labor movement kindled hope in 1980 with a courageous strike for better wages at the Lenin Shipyard. After a decade of battle—a struggle by any definition—Solidarity named a government to reshape Poland's economy. And early in 1990, at the shipyard in Gdansk where it all began, [wages were so low] a worker's average salary was a banana and a half an hour.

The Poles' rough-and-tumble economic reform had a simple point of departure. They would let market forces wreak havoc and then pick up the pieces. The [Polish monetary unit the] zloty was dashed on the rocks unmercifully. In October 1989 it was valued at 1,800 to the U.S. dollar. But people who wanted a real dollar paid 6,000 zlotys on the black market. In January banks gave a better rate than the black marketeers, 9,500 zlotys. Poland had a convertible currency. Poles could buy foreign currency with zlotys, but anyone with a fixed income, or a life's savings stashed in a mattress, teetered at the edge of ruin.

[Government] subsidies ended, and prices mushroomed out of all logic. One day it cost four times as much to use a public telephone, though it was still five calls for a penny. But fuel also quadrupled. Poles shivered at home and left their cars on the street. Only wages remained controlled. Meat was suddenly plentiful, but housewives could not afford it. Families did without bread. Bananas, a traditional barometer of well-being, were abundant. But a banana cost a quarter, and workers made forty cents an hour.

Waiting for promises to materialize, Poles knew they needed much more outside help than was coming. They could not pay even interest on a $40-billion Western debt. Despite a first rush of Western warmth—"Let Poland be Poland," Ronald Reagan had once said, without elaboration—Poles realized the free market did not operate on sympathy, or justice. An old elite held positions of economic power. Some people were getting much richer than others. Many got laid off. Poland's endemic stoicism took on a tinge of envy. Its trappings of capitalism included car thefts, beggars, and soup kitchens.

But, on a January morning, I went back to the Gdansk shipyard to ask workers what they thought of revolution. Roman Nurek, thirty-five, told me he was terrified that he might not be able to support his wife and infant daughter. Life, he said, was a struggle. I asked if the revolution was worth it. He looked at me like I was crazy. . . .

First Christmas in Forty-Three Years

In Romania, as in Czechoslovakia, there were those words again [*freedom* and *democracy*]. Young people tried them out, speaking them aloud. At the Bucharest Emergency Hospital, medical students clustered around me and, prompted by questions, probed at the words, freedom and democracy, as if they were dissecting exotic birds.

"What is it to live free, to travel free, to speak freely?" mused Ioana Popescu, "We have only seen dark and silence." A friend, Anda Preda, added, "We can't realize what freedom is. You grew up in freedom, and you do not realize what this means to us." She paused and apologized: "I've learned English eleven years, and this the first time I speak it."

Bogdan Lazaroae, who ended up translating for reporters, was sometimes as confused as the outsiders. "I am afraid people will ask me what I am doing with foreigners, but no one asks," he said. "That's a little bit of freedom. I am afraid to speak the name of Ceausescu in the street, maybe someone will tell me I'm an enemy, but they don't. That's a little bit of freedom."

The student doctors also had to define Christmas. This was December 24 and, for the first time in forty-three years, carols were played in public. "Maybe you can't understand what Christmas this year means for us," said Anda Preda. "You hear these Christmas songs every year, and you are used to them."

Ioana Popescu started to speak of family and joy but kept glancing up the corridor at men her own age bleeding from gunshot wounds. "Next year, we will have Christmas and freedom and know what they mean," she said. "Next year we will have Christmas."

The words were more tangible up the hill at the Metropolitan Cathedral. As Christmas approached, Romanians had come to thank God and their children for deliverance. One was a kindly mother named Victoria Ionita. She told a translator she was "very happy," but her eyes suggested that was a feeble understatement. "There were so many years when I did not come to church for fear of the government," she said. "Now there is shooting in the streets, but I come because of trust in God."

On the open cathedral porch, heat from so many thin yellow candles warmed the icy air. In silent knots, people waited in line to speak to three American reporters. It was as if we were at once their confessors and their conduit to a world they had just rejoined. Every eye was swollen and red. I noticed one man whose face strained to hold its composure. His features twitched and stiffened until he suddenly burst into uncontrollable sobs. Twenty years of guilt, shame, and suppressed anger let loose all at once. Like me, he was a journalist.

"All the things that I have seen and stood by silently for so many years," he began. "They have killed children, thousands." He spilled out memories of Ceausescu's atrocities. Coolly he described a process of censorship and mind control that might have shaken [English writer George] Orwell. Then he broke down again, repeating to me but mostly to himself, "I'm so sorry. I'm so happy."

A Call for Democracy

Mikhail Gorbachev

The Soviet Union had been ruled by an iron-fisted Communist power structure for almost seventy-five years. That regime was threatened in 1991, when Soviet leader Mikhail Gorbachev prepared to sign a historic agreement freeing the fifteen Soviet republics from Russian control. This would transfer powers over taxation, state security, and natural resources to local governments. Top Soviet generals, however, were not about to let the power structure of this country of more than 260 million people be dissolved with the stroke of Gorbachev's pen. On August 18, 1991, a special detachment of old-line Communist soldiers put Gorbachev under house arrest. The eight former military officers who were the coup leaders lamely announced to the world that Gorbachev was too old and sick to run the country.

Within hours resistance to the coup was organized with Boris Yeltsin as its leader. Yeltsin clamored onto a tank in front of the Russian White House and called for a general strike. By August 20, the streets of Moscow were filled with 150,000 protesters. As the coup leaders organized airplanes and paratroopers for an armed assault on the protesters, people locked arms to form a human chain around the White House where Yeltsin was staying. By the next day the resistance had won. With crowds cheering and soldiers waving revolutionary flags, Gorbachev returned to

Excerpted from *The August Coup*, by Mikhail Gorbachev (New York: Harper-Collins, 1991). Copyright ©1991 by Mikhail S. Gorbachev. Reprinted with permission from the Russian Author's Society, formerly VAAP.

power. Democracy had triumphed over Communism.

The former Soviet Union, however, still faced a host of incredibly complicated problems in transforming its Communist economy into one based on free market capitalism. It was a struggle that the people continued to confront for the rest of the decade and beyond.

Mikhail Sergeyevich Gorbachev was appointed general secretary of the Soviet Union in 1985, and in March 1990 he became the first democratically elected president of the USSR.

It is amazing, but every day since those three days in August seems at times like a week. I am finishing putting in order what I have said and thought since returning to Moscow from the south, and it is just a month since the beginning of the coup. Just a month, but how much has happened, how much has changed since then.

The attempted coup was crushed. The democrats are celebrating the victory, but life demands action. It demands carefully thought through and unorthodox actions. People are discontented with the fact that their daily life is so hard and that there are no changes for the better yet. Here lies the main danger. It was precisely that which the organizers of the coup wanted to exploit. That is why there is no time to lose. We must act, push forward with the process of reform and give people economic freedom, then they will themselves realize their potential. We have a great deal to learn. We have to learn to handle the politics, the economics and the life of the state. And in that respect the democrats are still weak.

All of us have a lot to learn, so as to govern within the framework of democracy, of political and in particular economic pluralism.

Otherwise people's patience will simply be exhausted. Then there would be an uncontrolled outburst of discontent and chaos—and then just expect the worst. No less dangerous for the realization of our plans would be a reaction resulting from the people's fatigue, the spread of frustration, indifference and apathy. This might simply stop our movement towards a market economy.

Three Major Problems

I would divide into three groups the whole bundle of acute problems with which we are now confronted. In the first place there are the current problems—of providing the population with food, of organizing the efficient functioning of the fuel and energy branch of the economy, and of meeting our needs in medicines. The second group of problems' concerns the creation of the conditions for the development of private enterprise and a decisive speeding up of the economic reforms. Only by proceeding in parallel in solving both groups of problems shall we be able to survive the winter and spring, obtain the desired effect from carrying out the reforms, and begin extracting ourselves from the crisis.

The most important thing now is how to survive to the spring, how to get through the winter. And all the rest, apart from these two groups of problems, is a matter of advancing more quickly to the free market and stimulating entrepreneurial activity.

But for the reforms to succeed people have to believe in them. Without people the reforms will not move off the ground, without their active participation everything will remain a dead letter. Or, on the other hand, there could be a backlash if living conditions become even worse. That would be a heavy blow struck at democracy.

I recall how, following my meeting in the Kremlin with the ambassador of the United States, I was returning to my office and was surrounded by people. We started to talk. Interestingly enough, no one was complaining about the difficulties. They said there were, of course, plenty of them, but that the people were ready to rally round, to withstand the test and support the policy of reform to the end.

Tremendous Possibilities

We have tremendous possibilities. That is not just a standard phrase, a cliché. I am hearing it said repeatedly by foreigners whom I talk to. They say: you have everything—an educated people and huge material resources—and you can become a rich country. Yes, we must become a rich country. I repeat: we have everything we need for that. We must change. Then we shall live differently.

More than anything else I think now about how our children and my grandchildren and those who are between fifteen and twenty today are going to live. It is in that that I see the sense of my efforts, because after all it was for them that it all started. We were not frightened off by the difficulties. We knew that we were facing a lot of complicated and difficult problems. We set ourselves the objective that, today already, people should join in the democratic process and feel themselves to be real people. . . .

But what has to change is also our way of life and living standards. I very much wish that the people who have given so much to this land should feel that their time has come at last—a happy time.

Now, when the future of our great country is being decided, I think least of all about myself. That is why it was both a difficult moment and at the same time it was easy for me to make a decision when the [coup] plotters presented their ultimatum. I made my choice long ago. Plotters can act without bothering about the means. But I cannot try to achieve my ends by other ways. . . . The choice of democracy makes it impossible for me to use any other methods. Otherwise there would inevitably be a repetition of the past, of everything we have condemned. However complicated the problems may be they must be resolved democratically. I see no other way but democracy.

Mass Destruction in Kosovo

Brian Duffy

When the cold war ended in 1990, most people imagined an end to conflict in Europe. But when the government of Yugoslavia collapsed, former Communist leader Slobodan Milosevic began a wave of Serbian terror that resulted in three wars in ten years. The slaughter began in Bosnia in April 1992, as hundreds of thousands of Muslims were killed in a genocidal purge called ethnic cleansing. Milosevic's murderous impulses culminated in 1999 when the Serbs rampaged through the province of Kosovo, raping women, pillaging towns and villages, and murdering ethnic Albanians who were a majority in the province. At least 1.5 million Albanians were driven from their homes, creating the worst European refugee crisis since World War II.

From March to June 1999, the NATO countries, led by the United States, waged an air war against Serbia, spending $2.6 billion to fly thirty-two thousand bomber missions that destroyed nine hundred targets. Over fifteen hundred civilians were killed as well as five thousand Serbian soldiers.

After the war, it was discovered that more than six hundred of Kosovo's eight hundred major towns and villages were badly damaged or destroyed by the Serbs, and the mass graves of thousands of men, women, and children were unearthed in at least eighty-five villages. Milosevic and several of his associates were charged with crimes against humanity by the war crimes tribunal in The Hague, Netherlands.

Excerpted from "The Art of the Deal," by Brian Duffy, *U.S. News & World Report,* June 14, 1999. Copyright © June 14, 1999 by U.S. News & World Report. Visit www.usnews.com for additional information.

A t the end, there was silence. For only the second time in the 11-week NATO bombing campaign against Yugoslavia, there was no overnight air-raid alert in Belgrade. Ordnance fell outside the capital, and NATO ground-attack jets continued to hunt Serbian forces in Kosovo. But the sudden quiet in Belgrade was eerie. Which was odd because, until the bombing began back in March, air-raid sirens hadn't been heard in Europe since the end of World War II. War is funny that way—distorting memory, compressing time. But if the agreement negotiated [the first week of July 1999] can hold, Europe bids fair now to end the century—a century that has seen 50 million of its men, women, and children killed in wars—with a fragile peace.

Kosovo has been an extraordinarily ugly little conflict. Thousands died. Thousands more were injured. More than 1.5 million Kosovars were driven from their homes, and most may have none to return to. As they did in the very early days of the century, the Balkans have shown their ability to spin Europe into murderous chaos. It's the very "Balkanness" of the conflict that makes so many so nervous about its sudden end. "It's the Balkans," shrugs one U.S. official. "You've got to be cautious.". . .

Three-Time Loser Milosevic

Ways must be found to return some 850,000 refugees who have fled Kosovo, to get help and food to thousands more who may be wandering homeless in the province now, and to guarantee their safety and security as Serbian troops withdraw. The rebel Kosovo Liberation Army must be persuaded to disarm, to refrain from attacking Serbian forces remaining in Kosovo, and to genuinely buy into the peace process.

Then, of course, there is the problem of Milosevic himself. A three-time loser who has now gone down to defeat in the third Balkan war he has started in the past decade, he essentially accepted NATO's terms for cessation of hostilities in Kosovo last week. But the place holds powerful sway over the man. Not only was he born in the province he has now managed to "cleanse" of its ethnic Albanian majority, but it is the key to his claim of leadership of the Serbs. To celebrate the 600th anniversary of the Battle of Kosovo on the legendary Field of Blackbirds, back in 1989, Milosevic led a swaggering procession to the province and addressed more than a million Serbs in denouncing Kosovo's Albanian majority. It was Milosevic's attacks on the Albanians that year that marked the first stage in the breakup of Yugoslavia, and NATO leaders are right to question whether he's really ready to relinquish his claims on the province after just a few months of bombing.

There appear to be at least two reasons for the decision. The first is tactical. Since the war's onset, Milosevic played a brilliant game of cat and mouse with NATO. Certain the alliance would crack in time, he counted on Yugoslav civilian casualties to force the issue. The way he did that was to keep his formidable antiaircraft weapons largely intact, refusing to fire up their radar so they could be targeted by NATO jets. That forced NATO brass to order pilots to release missiles and bombs from higher altitudes. That in turn caused targeting errors—a rest home, a hospital, and refugee convoys. But the alliance didn't crack.

Charged with Horrific Massacres

What happened instead was that . . . the highflying NATO jets were having very little luck attacking Milosevic's 40,000 troops and paramilitaries in Kosovo. But then something happened. The rebel Kosovo Liberation Army launched a ground attack from neighboring Albania into Kosovo. Milosevic's forces rallied to repulse the incursion, but in doing so their tanks and armored personnel carriers had to leave the redoubts where they had been hiding since the bombing began. They became sitting ducks. Of the 5,000 Serbian troop fatalities and perhaps twice that number wounded, NATO officials say, most occurred within the final days of the war.

The second reason Milosevic may have moved when he did is more complicated. After the International Criminal

Tribunal for the Former Yugoslavia indicted the Serbian leader on May 27, many worried that it made it impossible for NATO to cut a deal with him. The indictment makes for grisly reading. It charges Milosevic and four top aides with the murders of 340 ethnic Albanians and seven horrific massacres in Kosovo. "We'd drawn horns and a tail on Milosevic," says a White House official. The Serbian leader may not have cared terribly, but it does seem to have concentrated his mind, as did the growing talk of a NATO ground invasion.

By cutting a deal now, Milosevic remains in power, at least for the moment. But, more important, he remains in Serbia—beyond the reach of the war crimes tribunal and its investigators. All wars are plagued by mistakes and miscalculation. But in a conflict that seems to have been ruled by the law of unintended consequences to an extraordinary degree, the Milosevic indictment may have done more than millions of tons of NATO bombs to finally bring the Serbian leader to heel.

A War Fought for Moral Reasons

Whatever the reasons for Milosevic's decision, if he keeps to his word, it's an important victory. Milosevic's ethnic cleansing in a place most Americans had never heard of didn't engage important U.S. interests. But it may be the first war in U.S. history undertaken for almost exclusively moral reasons. And it wasn't just America that decided it was worth going to war. European leaders had stood by and watched Milosevic's earlier marauding in Bosnia and elsewhere in the Balkans, doing nothing. This time, working through NATO, they acted.

That it prevailed—if, in fact, it does prevail—sends a powerful signal. "NATO's success in Kosovo will be the biggest deterrent to tyrants the world over," British Prime Minister Tony Blair predicted, "and the biggest rallying call for democracy." No less an eminence than Singapore's Lee Kuan Yew (himself no slouch in the dictator department) agreed, noting recently that a NATO victory in Kosovo "will affect men's minds across the world.". . .

For President Clinton, the fruits of a successful conclusion in Kosovo cannot be overestimated. Critics of the venture, who have derided the NATO mission from the outset, were unbowed by Milosevic's concession last week. Rep. John Kasich, an Ohio Republican, called the Kosovo venture "a disaster" but urged acceptance of the Milosevic deal. Perennial Republican presidential candidate Patrick Buchanan weighed in with this: "Smashing a fifth-rate power that can't even defend itself? I think we should be ashamed of ourselves."

But those were the exceptions. Democrats hailed Clinton's commitment to challenge genocide and ethnic cleansing and said his faith in NATO's air campaign appears to have been vindicated. The big winner, of course, if the deal sticks, is Al Gore. He won't have to campaign against the backdrop of swelling tides of refugees and burning homes and hospitals in Belgrade.

There are still plenty of ifs, though. . . . To achieve a true peace, unlike the "cold peace" that now obtains in Bosnia, more must happen. Most important, Kosovo's refugees

must be allowed to "go home," as President Clinton said at the outset of the conflict. Among many things NATO war planners appear not to have understood before the bombing began is that Milosevic long ago made the creation of refugees an objective of his war policy, not a byproduct. And so it is that tens of thousands of Bosnia's refugees refused to return, knowing they are unwelcome there.

Will it be the same in Kosovo? Many say they want to go back, but it's too late to plant crops now, many homes and villages have been all but destroyed, and the prospect of a winter of starvation looms. A top U.S. official suggests that perhaps a fifth of the estimated 850,000 refugees now in camps will try to return immediately. If true, it would play havoc with the arrival of the 50,000 peacekeeping troops, not to mention the massive relief effort now being readied. But that's what may happen. A failure to assist as many refugees as want to return, and to fully provide for their needs while permanent shelter is erected for them, would do much to undermine the NATO effort in Kosovo. The effort is certain to cost billions.

CHAPTER 3

Violence in
the Land

AMERICA'S DECADES

Who Was to Blame for the Waco Disaster?

John Taylor

John Taylor, a journalist who wrote this article for *New York* magazine, gives an overview of the many figures who were implicated in the tragedy at the Branch Davidian compound in Waco, Texas. David Koresh and scores of his followers—including dozens of children—died in a fire while under siege from the FBI. Even before the smoke had cleared, harsh criticism was aimed at Attorney General Janet Reno, the FBI, the Bureau of Alcohol, Tobacco and Firearms (ATF), and President Bill Clinton in their handling of the matter. Others placed the blame squarely on Koresh for his apocalyptic religious beliefs.

It's hard to think of an activity more psychically luxuriant than second-guessing. It combines a maximum amount of self-righteous moral indignation with irresistible opportunities to display intellectual superiority, a license for the unlimited criticism of others, and absolutely no exposure to risk or responsibility. No wonder then that second-guessing of the FBI's attempt to end the standoff with the Branch Davidians reached a level of shrill ferocity well before the flames that destroyed the cult's compound were extinguished.

The original February 28 [1993] raid on the compound by agents of the Bureau of Alcohol, Tobacco, and Firearms

Excerpted from "The Waco Blame Game," by John Taylor in *Religious Cults in America*, edited by Robert Emmet Long (New York: The H.W. Wilson Company, 1994). Copyright ©1994 by The H.W. Wilson Company. Reprinted with permission from *New York* Magazine.

had unquestionably been bungled. That debacle created a narrative premise: that buffoonish Feds and crazed cult members were together acting out some sort of black farce in the trashy trailer-park-gothic setting of rural Texas. The premise was reinforced by subsequent developments. David Koresh's shameless greed for publicity, his biblical rantings, and his increasingly preposterous demands (a word processor to complete an analysis of the Seven Seals), combined with the surreal appearance of tanks and helicopters, with loudspeakers belting out "Jingle Bell Rock" and recordings of rabbits being slaughtered, while lawyers hawked book rights, made for a satirical techno-pop extravaganza.

The situation was far wilder than anything [movie director] Robert Altman ever dared to conceive. But just as it began to seem too ridiculous for words, it ended, abruptly and tragically. There was no time for mourning, however—except perhaps at a few church services in Waco—no letup in the overwrought media cyclone, and thus little opportunity for most people to pause and actually experience their feelings about the death by fire of 17 children and 69 adults. Instead, the farce of the standoff was immediately supplanted by the equally hysterical farce of, to use a phrase George Bush popularized [in 1992], "the blame game."

Could Tragedy Have Been Averted?

Some in the press approached this task with a gusto that bordered on joy. The idea about FBI culpability in the immolation of the cultists fulfilled not only the original narrative premise of the siege (bumbling Feds) but also the more general, reflexive skepticism liberal journalists have had of federal law-enforcement agents. The tradition, ever since the sixties, has been to romanticize outlaws while disparaging the FBI as an enemy of social progress, the very embodiment of reactionary authority. Its members were all thought to wear black Corfam shoes and white socks. Their malice was supposed to be exceeded only by their incompetence. In Waco, according to those who subscribed to this view, they had once again made utter fools of themselves.

While most of the public, in an initial poll, agreed with Bill Clinton that David Koresh had killed his followers, the members of the press tended to blame the FBI. The Bureau had "provoked" Koresh, they felt. It had "triggered" his action. Koresh, after all, couldn't be held responsible because he was insane, and his followers couldn't be held responsible because they were in his thrall. If the FBI had treated Koresh with the patience and understanding that the insane deserve, the tragedy could have been averted.

Instead, federal agents, in a fit of macho pique because he had successfully thwarted them, *drove* the cult leader to start the fire. In this scenario, Koresh becomes almost as much a victim as the children, his decision to ignite the compound an incidental act in a series of events he did not initiate. (It seems safe to assume, despite denials from the survivors, that Koresh did burn the place down. Federal agents saw people apparently lighting the fire. It seemed to begin in several places, and engulfed the entire building almost immediately.)

A Pretext to Destroy Himself

But what was in fact incidental to the tragic outcome was the FBI's decision to take action. It merely provided Koresh with the pretext he had been looking for to destroy himself and his followers. The idea that Koresh could have been talked into surrendering at some point in the future is not supported by the facts. He and his followers knew they had murdered four federal agents and wounded sixteen others. They were aware that if they surrendered, the cult would be broken up, many of them would be given long prison terms, and, since this was Texas, a few would probably be sentenced to death and executed. That clearly had no appeal.

What did seem appealing was an indefinite state of siege. It invested the cultists' daily routine with intensity and satisfied their collective persecution complex. Their attitude toward the federal agents who surrounded them was increasingly casual, almost blasé; cultists, who had kept indoors after the first shoot-out, took to strolling outside the compound walls and appearing on the roof to smoke cigarettes. The discomfort they endured was minimal. They had, according to the FBI, up to two years' supply of food. They had their own source of water. They had their 104 assault rifles, their grenade launcher, their 8,000 rounds of ammunition.

Many of the cultists' relatives have faulted the FBI for not arranging for them to talk to their family members inside the compound, but it's highly unlikely that Koresh would have allowed his followers to get on the telephone with their relatives, who would encourage them to desert. A cult leader's hold over his followers exists in inverse proportion to their contacts with the rest of society.

It is true that if the FBI had not moved in on April 19, the cultists and their children would be alive today. But because that date had a certain arbitrariness does not mean the decision to take action was wrong. Such specifics almost always have an arbitrary quality. The alternative was not to take action on some less arbitrary occasion—since Koresh was becoming more erratic and the talks with him were regressing rather than progressing, the prospects for a negotiated settlement were dwindling—but to take no action.

That would have been the advice of the cult experts who, in the days after the conflagration, faulted the FBI for failing to consult with *them*. But the ensuing standoff could have lasted as long as two years. It would have allowed Koresh to flout the country's laws, setting up his own rogue kingdom within the national borders. And it, too, could just as easily have ended in tragedy. "Do we wait 90 more days until the children died?" asked Jeff Jamar, the FBI agent in charge of the siege. "How would the federal government look when we finally get into the compound [if] there are children dying of hunger, children dying of disease because of the conditions?"

On a Rescue Mission?

In the accusatory deluge that has followed the fire, it's been easy to forget that the federal agents were on a rescue mission. While they did not have, as they first suggested, a sheaf of new reports of child abuse, they nonetheless had legitimate reason to be alarmed about the children. The old reports were persuasive. And conditions in the compound were unsanitary. According to Justice Department spokesman Carl Stern, human waste was being thrown out the compound doors in pails.

The charge has been made that the FBI acted out of "impatience," suggesting that judgment had lapsed into emotionalism. In fact, agents showed restraint throughout the operation. They adhered to the policy of "no return fire," even though as they moved in on the compound, the cultists fired some 80 rounds at them.

Attorney General Janet Reno has admitted that everyone failed to anticipate the mass suicide. But failure to anticipate someone's decision to commit suicide does not translate into responsibility for it. That Koresh was intent all along on killing himself and his followers and their children if he had to leave the compound is evident from the fact that this is what occurred. As happened in Jonestown, it was the unavoidable dissolution of the cult, brought on by the crimes committed at the leader's instigation, that led the leader to order the death of his followers. Some of them, according to reports circulating in Waco, may have been killed by Koresh's "Mighty Men" before the fire started.

The tank muzzle punching through the flimsy compound wall was only the proximate cause of the catastrophe. The FBI's mistakes were procedural rather than fundamental. If its agents are truly guilty of anything, it is the guilt of those unable to prevent the inevitable.

Horror in Oklahoma City

Clive Irving

On April 19, 1995, at 9:02 A.M., Timothy McVeigh, an acknowledged member of the militia movement, planted a car bomb near the Alfred P. Murrah Federal Building in downtown Oklahoma City. The bomb ripped a nine-story hole in the building and killed 168 people, many of them children. The people who lived through that day—both the survivors and the rescuers—will never forget those moments that turned part of downtown Oklahoma City into a scene reminiscent of a battlefield.

Clive Irving is a journalist in London and New York and is the senior consulting editor of *Condé Nast Traveler.*

The first report of an explosion came from a police patrol car in the downtown area. Within seconds, the police and fire department radio channels erupted with calls. All over Oklahoma City people felt the force of a blast. Some thought it was a sonic boom; others a gas explosion. Those who were trained to respond to an emergency—doctors, nurses, police, firemen—dropped whatever they were doing and tried to find out if they were needed. Some heard radio reports; others saw the first live television pictures. As police and firemen located the site of the explosion, the scale of the devastation astounded them. Nobody comprehended the cause, but the carnage

---

was clear and terrible on the streets. The focus was the block framing the Alfred P. Murrah Federal Building—between Fourth and Fifth streets, east to west, and Harvey and Robinson, north to south. When rescuers converged on this area, they found what they later recalled as "organized chaos." Within a pattern of trained responses, hundreds of individual acts of heroism and initiative—dealing with grim life-or-death decisions—were carried out in the first hour. What follows are the accounts of survivors of the blast and those who formed the impromptu rescue and medical teams. Their own words are interspersed with flashes from the police and fire department radio channels.

Clark C. Peterson was at work in his office on the fourth floor of the Murrah Building at 9:02:

At about 8:58 A.M., I sat three feet from the north windows as my supervisor gave me final instructions for a project. I returned to my desk, which was about twenty feet south of the windows, and began to type. At about 9:02 A.M., an electric spark appeared by my computer and everything turned black. Propelled objects raced throughout the darkness amid the sound of moaning metal.

I caught a glimpse of a terrified girl with both arms straight up in the air. We were apparently falling, but I did not realize what had happened until a minute or two later. The sight of her was so brief and faint that I could not identify her. She yelled, "Ah!" as if there were not enough time to inhale air.

I was calm throughout; everything changed to a deadlike settling of debris amid the black atmosphere. As the blackness and dust began to clear, I discovered that the armchair I was seated in had been replaced. I remained in a sitting position, but on a flat, ceilinglike material, which was on top of a three-story pile of rubble.

I saw the north half of the Murrah Building was gone, except for the east and west sides. I was ten feet in front of the remaining structure, about level with the third floor. "This had to be a bomb!" I thought, and a twenty-foot crater below confirmed that it was. I could not see anybody else in the building or rubble.

Sergeant Jerry Flowers is with the Oklahoma City Police Gang Unit. He was one of the first on the scene:

At 9:02 A.M. I was in the Police Academy discussing training. The academy building shook. Major Steve Upchurch yelled down the hallway that the Federal Building downtown had just blown up. Sergeant Steve Carson, Sergeant Don Hull, and I put on our police raid jackets. I drove to Fourth Street close to Hudson, where we were forced to stop because of debris. We ran toward the Murrah Building. Black smoke was shooting in the air. People, both old and young, were covered with blood. Some were holding towels and clothing articles against their bodies trying to stop the bleeding. Babies and adults were lying on the sidewalks. Some appeared to be dead and some alive. Everywhere I looked was blood, misery, and pain. One lady sat on a curb holding a blood-soaked shirt against her head while a stream of blood ran down her chest. What touched me about her was that she was trying to console a small girl, about eight years old, whose hair was matted with blood and gray dust. I've never seen so much pain, both physical and emotional.

Steve Carson and I ran to the north side of the Federal Building. I saw a car hood burning in the top of a tree. Debris, rocks, bodies, burned cars, glass, fire, and water covered Fifth Street. A large hole about thirty feet in diameter was where a small circle drive used to be in front of the Murrah Building, used by handicapped motorists. As we approached the northwest corner of the building, I could see a small hole where rescue workers were going into the building. Sergeant Bob Smart with the OCPD Robbery Detail was yelling, "Let's get these people out." Steve and I ran into the rubble and were handed a board stretcher that had a middle-aged man on it. He was covered with blood and his clothes were mostly torn off. It was obvious that he was dead. We passed this man to the outside of the building. I never saw him again. . . .

POLICE: Bring All Fire
and Ambulances You Can Get

Sergeant Jerry Flowers: Steve and I went through a small door. The floor went drastically downhill. Water came up over the top of my boots and the dust nearly prevented us from breathing. It was very dark as we crawled over large pillars of concrete just to get to an area where we could hear people yelling for help. We made our way into a room where large slabs of concrete were lying from one floor down to the next. There was a large hole you could look up through and see the nine broken floors hanging above our heads. Large ropes of steel rebar hung down and others protruded from the floor where we were trying to walk.

People were yelling for help. Our vision was impaired by darkness and dust. One lady was imprisoned under a huge slab of concrete and rebar, yelling to rescue workers not to leave her. I reached between the rebar and rock, patting her back and telling her we would get her out. Firefighters swarmed into the room. A generator was started and portable lights lit up the area we were in. As firefighters started to cut the steel to free the woman, we heard another cry. Looking down into what appeared to be a well, we saw a lady trapped on her back by concrete. The floor around her was filling up with water. She kept yelling, "Don't let me drown." Rescuers attacked the well to free the woman and were successful. . . .

Brad Lovelace is a police officer with the Oklahoma Capital Patrol. Within minutes of the explosion, he began searching the YMCA Building, to the northeast of the Federal Building:

I came to a room that terrified me. Although it was damaged extensively, I could tell that fifteen minutes earlier it had been a functioning day-care center. Thoughts of my two small daughters rushed through my head. I yelled out, "Is anyone in here?" I found nothing and heard no one, so I moved on and at approximately 9:30 A.M., my efforts were rewarded. In the corner of the basement, I saw three little girls huddled up together. They were obviously in shock and could not speak. I told them they were going to be fine and asked them their names, but it seemed as though they were not even listening. The girls were between ages four and six. They were too big for me to carry all three upstairs at once, so I picked up the two smallest girls and told the eldest that I would be right back to get her. Immediately, her daze was gone and tears welled up in her eyes. I got down on my knees, at face level with her, and said, "I promise I'll be back." She nodded. I carried the two smaller girls up the stairs and out to the triage center. When I returned to the basement, the older girl was still in the same spot waiting for me. When she saw me, she said nothing and didn't smile, but put her arms out toward me. I picked her up, carried her out, and went back to the YMCA to finish my search. . . .

Heather Taylor is a college student majoring in basic emergency medical technology. She arrived early at the scene with Dr. Carl Spengler:

My adrenaline was the only thing that was keeping me going, because I hadn't slept for twenty-four hours and I didn't realize how serious the situation was. I heard some people screaming, and ran over to this man who looked just like my grandfather. The man had severe lacerations on his scalp and neck, from falling glass. He was still breathing and was awake. He was shaking, a sign of shock. Dr. Spengler checked his lung sounds and yelled real loud, "Take a deep breath."

I left Dr. Spengler to see about a police officer who had fallen. He was lying on the ground, screaming that his back was burning. . . . I was the only trained rescue worker there. I grabbed a C collar. I was yelling at the cop to hold still, since he probably had a cervical-spinal injury. I placed the collar on him. Someone got a long spine board and we strapped him to it and an ambulance took him away.

I realized that I didn't have any personal protective equipment on, and the scene was not safe and secure. We are taught that paramedics are not useful if they are dead paramedics. So I grabbed some gloves and gave some to the doctor. While I was putting them on, I looked up and saw a man walking on what was left of the third floor. I told Dr. Spengler that we needed to get him down because he was missing his right arm. While the fire department worked to get him down, we decided to see what the other side of the building was like.

The south side of the building was the worst. Dr. Spengler decided we needed to set up the triage (an area where

Antiterrorism Legislation

Author Tricia Andryszewski describes how, in the aftermath of the tragedy in Oklahoma City, Congress passed antiterrorism legislation that gave the government a host of new powers.

In April 1996, just in time for the first anniversary of the Oklahoma City bombing, Congress passed and President Clinton signed into law a final version of the antiterrorism legislation crafted in response to the bombing. The major provisions of the bill included:

• Allotment of up to $1 billion over four years for the federal government to spend fighting terrorism;

• Requirement that criminals in many federal cases make restitution to their victims;

• More power for the federal government to exclude or deport foreigners suspected of ties to terrorists or convicted of other crimes;

• More power for the federal government to prosecute U.S. citizens who raise money for groups that participate in terrorism, even if the money is used for legal activities;

• Requirement that manufacturers of plastic explosives (but not the fertilizer used in the Oklahoma City bombing) mix microscopic "taggants" into their products so they can be traced;

victims are given priority according to their condition), since no one else was doing it. More and more people started to arrive with the equipment we needed. This was the moment when I got scared. Dr. Spengler gave me triage tags and told me to follow him around and tag the people minor, moderate, critical, or dead. You would think that you wouldn't waste your time on the dead, but tagging the dead kept people from going back to them and trying to save them.

• Establishment of sharp limits on "habeas corpus" rights, limiting the ability of prisoners, especially those on death row, to appeal their convictions or sentences to higher courts.

Civil liberties activists strongly objected to the legislation, claiming that it would seriously erode the free-speech and free-association rights of U.S. citizens. Furthermore, they said, while it would have little effect on determined terrorists, it would have a disastrous effect on innocent prisoners wrongly incarcerated for unrelated crimes, as it would strictly limit their access to the courts.

In an unusually swift move, the U.S. Supreme Court agreed just days after the legislation became law to review whether several of its provisions were permitted by the U.S. Constitution. In June, the court unanimously affirmed that one of the law's provisions on federal court appeals by state prisoners was permitted. But other legal issues raised by the antiterrorism legislation remained unresolved. Several additional provisions of the law slowly made their way through the lower courts to an expected Supreme Court review. Congress considered even more antiterrorism legislation in response to the July 1996 explosions aboard TWA Flight 800 off Long Island, New York, and at a park near Olympic Games venues in Atlanta, Georgia.

Tricia Andryszewski, *The Militia Movement in America*. Brookfield, CT: Millbrook, 1997.

On the curb outside the building, the wounded were lined up. If they were talking, I tagged them minor; if they were bleeding severely, I tagged them moderate; if they were unconscious, I tagged them critical; and if they were not breathing, I tagged them dead.

As the firemen were bringing out the wounded, I tagged the first child dead. I heard someone tell me there was once a day care on the second floor. After that, I found myself making a temporary morgue—some call it "the church." A priest had arrived, and he followed right behind me, praying for the lost ones. The firemen were bringing out so many dead. As soon as I would take one child, another child was laid next to it. I remember one man, a bystander who was helping me, said, "Why all of the children, why?" I just watched him cry.

Then I heard the doctor calling my name, so I went to him. They had pulled a lady from the rubble. She was unconscious, she was missing her left foot, her right hand had been amputated, and her mandible was crushed. As Dr. Spengler was intubating her (putting a breathing tube through the mouth into the lungs), I was writing everything down and tagged her critical.

I went to the next victim pulled from the rubble, a woman in her twenties. She was unresponsive. I had been told that she was pregnant. As I was tying her down to the long spine board, I noticed that both of her legs had been crushed severely. After I tagged her, she was transported. Later I heard that she had died.

Our first priority was to establish a triage team. Dr. Spengler got on the intercom of the fire truck and told everyone to listen. I was amazed at how he took charge of the situation and everyone listened to him. He told everyone that he wanted twenty paramedics, twenty physicians, and twenty ICU nurses. He looked at me and said that I was to stay with him wherever he went. I just nodded.

Dr. Spengler instructed the firemen to let me tag all the victims coming out of the building. Since most of the victims brought out of the building were dead, I just made the tags out to read "Dead—Dr. Spengler," then I signed my initials. About six more dead children were brought out. I said a little prayer for them as I tagged them.

I will never forget my experience with this horrible tragedy. As I start my career in emergency medicine, nothing I will do will ever compare. I did learn I can make a difference.

Threats from the Militia Movement

Kenneth S. Stern

Kenneth S. Stern is America's leading expert on the militia movement and the author of five books on the subject. Stern has been tracking hate groups for more than a decade and the militia movement since its inception.

In this selection Stern concludes that by the mid-1990s an estimated fifteen thousand men and women had joined hundreds of different militia groups in forty states. Stern's research determined that members of these militias held beliefs ranging from the mainstream (the government overreacted at Ruby Ridge) to the bizarre (the government is training inner-city gang members to fight militia members). On a national level, Stern found militias using faxes, shortwave radios, videotapes, and the Internet, to share their information and warfare training exercises. Stern also discovered that in some rural areas, militia members threaten government officials and intimidate those who do not share their beliefs. One such person was Timothy McVeigh, convicted Oklahoma City bomber, who had close ties to a Michigan militia group.

T he well-armed and dangerous anti-government militia movement has been spreading with lightning pace across the country. Organizations and researchers who

---

monitor this movement maintain that militias have either direct or indirect connections with organized white supremacists and are using the Internet, faxes, national shortwave radio, and videotapes to share their information and warfare training exercises. The militias constitute a new manifestation of violent hate-group activity that does not target only the traditional victims—racial and religious minorities—but any representative of government or anyone perceived as opposing the militia and, therefore, seen as doing "the work of government." Militia members on the Internet claimed they were going to march on Washington and arrest Congress at gunpoint. An alert was issued by one group calling not only for the arrest of members of Congress, but also their "trial for Treason by Citizen Courts." According to the *Arizona Republic*, "a militia group obtained the names and home addresses of all federal officers [in Mississippi], prompting U.S. agencies to post a nationwide alert."

Some estimates suggest that there are more than 15,000 people connected with the militia movement in over 40 states. People associated with militias have shot at police officers; gathered to try to down a National Guard helicopter; and been arrested in armed confrontations (one in an armed raid on a courthouse by people whose accomplices were waiting outside with assault rifles with bayonets, thousands of rounds of ammunition, radio equipment, plastic handcuffs, and $80,000 in cash, gold and silver, as well as bogus $3 bills with President Clinton's portrait; and calmly explained how they might need to kill government officials.

Vocal Minority Dictating Public Policy

Even after such acts, militia members apparently feel comfortable enough to have their meeting notices listed in local papers. A Montana mayor aligned with this movement even declared his town a "freeman enclave" and then deposited $20,000,000 in bogus "freeman" money in a local bank. The threat of militia violence has frightened citizens away from participating in the political process. A Montana newspaper reports that "Some residents, fearing for their safety, have stopped attending [land use and other community] meetings altogether, allowing a vocal minority to dictate public policy." Mike Murray, a county commissioner in Montana, indicates that "We were . . . advised by law enforcement authorities that it's not wise to have our addresses listed in the phone book. . . . Sadly, people who want to be involved in government are being discouraged from participating, so we're losing the best and brightest we've got." A member of a California militia told his audience, "If your board of supervisors tries to do something you don't like, show up. They're going to assume someone in the back has a rope."

Some militias maintain they have connections to local law enforcement and military personnel, and say they are training with heavy weaponry stolen from U.S. military installations. Because militias are a threat to law and order, because they are organized around the country and are using the national communication systems for organizing, it is imperative that this movement not be viewed as a localized problem, but as a national one.

White supremacist and anti-Semite John Trochmann formed the Militia of Montana in February, 1994. Since then, similar groups, directly or indirectly connected to the white supremacist movement, have cropped up around the country. Hundreds of people have attended meetings, even in small communities. Many of these, including truck drivers, accountants, housewives, lawyers, farmers, doctors, loggers, and barbers, are preparing to fight the government because they believe their freedom is at stake.

Bizarre Conspiracy Theories

Cited among their reasons are claims that the government laid siege to the Branch Davidians at Waco and attacked white supremacist Randy Weaver in [Ruby Ridge,] Idaho, as well as that the United Nations is expanding its military role. They oppose the Brady Bill. ("Gun control is for only one thing," militia members insist, "people control.") Some speak of government plans to shepherd dissidents into 43 concentration camps. (Mysterious numbers on the back of road signs, some say, are for this purpose, or for providing information to invading troops.)

Others claim that the government plans to murder more than three-quarters of the American people; that unmarked black helicopters are poised to attack them and sometimes threaten people by focusing lasers into their eyes; that Hong Kong policemen and Gurka troops are training in the Montana wilderness in order to "take guns away from Americans" on orders from the Clinton Administration; that UN equipment is being transported on huge trains and Russian and German trucks are being shipped to attack Americans; that international traffic symbols are used in the U.S. as a tool for foreign armies so they will be able to move easily through the country; that there is a plot to give the North Cascade range in Washington State to the UN and the CIA; that urban street gangs, like the Bloods and Crips are being trained as "shock troops" for the New World Order; that military troops are lining up to invade on the Canadian border; that the Federal government has implanted computer chips in government employees to monitor citizens; that "those who want to take over the world are changing the weather"; that [former] House Speaker Newt Gingrich is part of a global conspiracy to create a one-government New World Order; and that, on a specific date, the government is going to raid militias around the country.

Targeting Minorities, Environmentalists, and Government Officials

The researchers who track militias believe that anti-Semitism is the philosophical basis on which much of this movement rests. (It claims that Jews and "international Jewish bankers" are behind a repressive New World Order.) The idea of ordinary people being victimized by secret government conspiracies reflects the tenor, if not the content, of the notorious anti-Semitic tract, *The Protocols of the Elders of Zion*. Nonetheless, the targets of the more extreme militia groups are not exclusively, or even primarily, Jews or other minorities.

Environmentalists also are vilified. Most despised are government officials. The Southern Poverty Law Center reports that a court clerk in California was pistol-whipped by militia members because she wouldn't file one of their Posse Comitatus–like writs. According to the Rural Organizing Committee, elected officials on the local level have been forced by armed militia members who pack their meetings to enact ordinances they know are illegal, under threat of death. It is alleged that some county officials have been intimidated into forgoing re-election, potentially leaving the field open to white supremacists.

A few local elected officials have supported the militias. State Senator Charles Duke of Colorado claimed that U.S. Sen. Hank Brown (R.-Colo.) is "owned" by Washington special interests. "I think [Brown] should be very careful when he comes back to the state. Most of Colorado is armed." Idaho Secretary of State Pete Cenerussa—at a meeting where a militia leader told his audience that "there will be blood in the streets" if a judge issues an order restricting access to a forest—said that Idaho "was planning to confer legal status on the militia once it reaches 10,000 members." On the other hand, some local newspapers are starting to editorialize against politicians legitimizing the militia movement.

Even though the quantity and quality of conspiracy theories and bigoted views may vary from militia to militia, they all share an anti-government animus. That paranoid stance—that the Federal government is criminal and that militia members are protecting the Constitution—is not to be underestimated. One possible explanation for this new phenomenon is that, since the fall of the Soviet Union and the end of the Cold War, the focus of the extreme right has been directed toward the American government. Jews are seen by many of the leaders of this movement—who share their ideology with new recruits who might have been attracted initially by issues like the Brady Bill—as the evil force behind government.

These militia members are not talking about change from the ballot box alone. Many are enamored by the prospect of change through bullets, explosives, and heavy armaments. It is not unreasonable to surmise that this blend of anti-Semitic and anti-government paranoia and guns will result in tragedies such as the bombing of the Federal Building in Oklahoma City in April, 1995, perpetrated by individuals who carry their beliefs to the extreme. This is a movement with an ideology of contempt for the government, including criminal laws.

Conducting Business in a Climate of Fear

It is urgent that law enforcement agencies understand the threat and begin to share strategies and information. Militia activity is not provided for by the Second Amendment. Private militias are in violation of paramilitary training laws, state constitutional provisions that reserve the right to form a militia to the state, and possibly other provisions of state and federal law. In the words of Ken Toole, president of the Montana Human Rights Network, "We can't conduct public business in an atmosphere of fear."

That fear is exemplified by a 1995 resolution of the Idaho legislature finding that "public statements threatening civil war and the infliction of bodily harm upon public officials are outside the realm of [First Amendment] rights." On the grass-roots level across the country, the militia movement is harassing its opponents, threatening law enforcement officials, stockpiling weapons, and spreading paranoid rumors on the Internet. It is time that state and Federal officials understand not only the danger of this movement, but also, from a more parochial vantage point, that government employees across the country are going about their tasks while there are people planning just when to target them in their cross-hairs. These individuals prepared to shoot at the slimmest indication of government actions. They may believe that the firefighter coming to put out the suspicious blaze in their barn or the member of the Forest Service counting rainbow trout in a nearby creek are part of an invasion force.

Laws must be enforced and, where not in place, enacted to make organized armed militias illegal. All people have a right to state their claims and organize in the marketplace of ideas. No one has the right to intimidate others with a choking atmosphere of fear, violence, and threats.

Killings on Campus

Neal Gabler

Neal Gabler is the author of several books detailing Holly-wood's influence on American culture. In the following se-lection Gabler takes on the killings in Columbine High School in Littleton, Colorado, concluding that the media had a lot to do with the tragedy. As police piece together the details of the fifth—and bloodiest—American school yard shooting in two years, Gabler questions the widespread lack of values that could make such a mass killing possible.

O f all the bizarre sidelights to the horrifying massacre at Columbine High School in Littleton, Colo., Tues-day, the most bizarre may have been the story of the stu-dents trapped inside the school who called local TV sta-tions on their cell phones and provided brief commentaries on the action. According to one report, they signed off only because they feared the intruders might be watching television themselves and thus discover the whereabouts of the cell-phone users. All of which suggests that even for the perpetrators and their victims, television was the great mediator.

By now, this is hardly surprising. Like so many real-life dramas in America, the Littleton tragedy became a media event even before the smoke had cleared and anyone knew what was really happening. Copters buzzed overhead, re-porters swarmed the scene and commentators were soon

Excerpted from "Becoming Your Fantasy in Virtual Munich Beer Hall," by Neal Gabler, *Los Angeles Times*, April 25, 1999. Reprinted with permission from the *Los Angeles Times*.

delivering sententious analyses of what it all meant, giving us a sense of *déjà vu*.

But tragedies like this are media events not only because the media immediately latch onto them. Often they are media events in two far more important senses: first, because the perpetrators usually seem to have modeled their behavior after certain figures in the popular culture; and, second, because the rampages seem ultimately to have been staged for the media on the assumption that if you kill it, they will come. Or, put another way, what we witnessed at Littleton was not just inchoate rage. It was a premeditated performance in which the two gunmen roamed the school dispatching victims, whooping with delight after each murder. Without pop culture, the slaughter would have been unimaginable.

Begin with the killers. In the inevitable post-mortems that follow these horrors, it was reported that the outcasts Dylan Klebold and Eric Harris were part of a high-school clique whose members wore long black trench coats and which dubbed itself the Trench Coat Mafia, a cinematic image if ever there was one. They were also devotees of the computer games "Doom" and "Quake," in which players prowl virtual hallways shooting virtual victims with virtual guns. They worshiped Adolf Hitler, loved Goth music and had a special fondness for Marilyn Manson, the mordant rockstar whose satanic persona is designed to scandalize parents of his fans. In short, Harris and Klebold were creatures of pop culture.

Saturated with Media Imagery

Given how much these two seemed to have been shaped by movies, music and computer games, it is tempting to blame the media once again for providing guidance to young would-be sociopaths and to call for greater responsibility from those who command our pop culture. But there have always been alienated teenagers, and the media have always supplied models for them, often violent ones, and yet most of them managed to resist emulating the violence. In

© Jerry Barnett for *The Indianapolis News*. Reprinted with permission.

fact, many observers have argued that the media may have had the opposite effect: letting us displace our anger rather than vent it. Disaffected teenagers in the 1950s and '60s had James Dean, Marlon Brando and Elvis Presley to give their rebelliousness form and help channel it. Disaffected teenagers in the '90s have Leonardo DiCaprio, "Stone Cold" Steve Austin and Manson.

Still, there is a real difference between then and now, and the difference is not the kinds of figures teenagers idolize; it is the kind of consciousness one brings to idolizing them. In the past, one may have identified with pop icons and affected their look and attitude, but few of us were deluded enough to think we could actually become Brando or Presley. We appropriated from them; we didn't see their reality converging with ours. They were "up there" on the screen. We were "down here" in real life. Never the twain shall meet.

What has been eroded is that distinction between the fantastic and the real. America is now so saturated with images that it seems we live within them, helpless to distinguish the genuine from the fabricated, the real from the confected. Life itself has become an entertainment medium, where the distance between "up there" and "down here" has closed considerably and where we feel empowered to be whatever we want, as Klebold and Harris so unspeakably demonstrated.

Children with Little Identity

One reason teens of the past may have been better able to distinguish between having fantasies and actualizing them was that their own reality may have been more firmly rooted in a sense of place. It may be no coincidence that many of the recent school shootings occurred in relatively new communities like Littleton and Springfield, Ore., where malls and houses were sprouting rapidly, or in declining communities like West Paducah, Ky., where the verities were under siege. It may be too simple to say that rootless, malleable communities with little identity of their own, save the identity stamped on them by mass culture, give rise to rootless, malleable children with little identity of their own, save the identity borrowed from mass culture, but it may not be too far off, either.

As for malleability, patching together a role from bits of pop culture, Harris and Klebold became part James Dean, part "Doom": alienated teens with an attitude. Having found their role, they then wrote a script for it. Decked out in their trench coats, they would enter the school and blast away as they had seen countless heroes do in countless movies, always with a *bon mot* to the defeated. "What are you whining about?" one was supposed to have said to terrified students. "You'll all be dead soon, anyway."

What helped give these fantasies body is yet another new instrument of the entertainment age: the Internet. Movies provided a personal reverie for those disaffected teenagers of the past, a dream they harbored alone in the sanctuary of their rooms. The Internet, where Harris had a Web page, has taken those personal dreams of power and the lost souls who dream them and collectivized them, creating a virtual Munich Beer Hall [where Hitler first attempted to use force to gain power] where anger feeds anger, hate feeds hate. With the Internet to connect them, teenagers are no longer silent sufferers. They can martial their suffering in cyberspace to realize it in real space.

Winning Media Stardom

To what end? Harris and Klebold were nobodies in a high-school world where, as always, the attention went to the athletic and the attractive. Columbine High even had closed-circuit TV that, by one account, kept recycling the exploits of the school's athletic teams and, in doing so, kept stoking the anger of the misfits outside the charmed circle. Gunning down athletes was clearly the misfits' revenge against the system that ignored them. But it was more. This particular revenge fantasy was devised, incredibly, to win its protagonists media stardom, to wrest from national television what they couldn't get from their own closed-circuit TV.

The sad fact is, their scheme worked. Everyone now knows the names Harris and Klebold. Journalists ransack their pasts to find motives, their pictures stare out at us from every newspaper and magazine and their words are immortalized. They are celebrities: the writers, directors and stars of a highly successful show that, for the time being, is the talk of the nation.

Unfortunately, in a country where celebrity so often trumps other values, they are likely to be mentors as well. Wherever there is an alienated teen whose sense of estrangement is reified by the Internet and energized by media models, there is a potential Littleton. Wherever there is a lonely teenager who desires the sanctification of the media to compensate for his own feelings of powerlessness, there is a potential Littleton.

When you live within a virtual reality, you have to expect some addled individuals won't accept the difference between the movie or video screen and the screen of life. But don't blame the media. Blame the general condition of modern American life that confuses realms so thoroughly that killing villains in "Doom" and killing children in a school cafeteria can seem pretty much the same, save for the fame the latter bestows.

CHAPTER 4

Racial and Gender Conflicts

AMERICA'S DECADES

Gender Issues in Black and White

Nellie Y. McKay

In 1991, the most liberal judge on the Supreme Court—and the only African American—Thurgood Marshall, 83, announced his retirement. George Bush quickly nominated a young, black judge named Clarence Thomas with strong conservative beliefs. When Thomas came before the Democratically controlled Senate, he stirred up a political storm over race and the rightward movement of the Court. But in the end, it was a story told by Anita Faye Hill—a woman who had previously worked for Thomas—that captured the country's attention.

Hill accused Thomas of sexual harassment and claimed that Thomas harassed her repeatedly in degrading and embarrassing ways that she felt powerless to stop. On October 15, 1991, after great national controversy, Thomas was confirmed on a 52–48 vote by the full Senate. Once he was on the bench, he became one of the Court's most staunchly conservative judges. But the allegations against him laid bare a gulf in male-female relations in Washington, where the corridors of power have always been dominated by men.

The harsh questioning of Anita Hill before the all-male panel of senators galvanized women voters, who in 1992 elected a record number of female candidates for Congress, a fact that led reporters to call the election "The Year of the Woman." After the Thomas-Hill hearings, complaints of

Excerpted from "Remembering Anita Hill and Clarence Thomas," by Nellie Y. McKay, in *Race-ing Justice and En-Gendering Power,* edited by Toni Morrison (New York: Pantheon Books, 1992). Copyright © by Nellie Y. McKay. Reprinted with permission from the author.

sexual harassment in the workplace skyrocketed. The Anita Hill episode was given credit for this trend.

Nellie Y. McKay teaches Afro-American and American literature at the University of Wisconsin, Madison, and has written about issues concerning black women and men, feminism, and multicultural education.

It was over in a few days, coming like a hurricane that whipped across the landscape of our lives, leaving a trail of wreckage and a less immediately apparent rainbow in its wake. On the surface of our busy days, the obscene spectacle ended, the shouting died down, newspaper editorial writers and op-ed–page columnists found more pressing subjects to pursue, and the almost unbridled fury that exploded from the nominee during the latter part of the Clarence Thomas Supreme Court confirmation hearings, in response to Anita Hill's allegations of sexual harassment against him, subsided into calm. In what appeared a return to business as usual, over the protests of many (though not the majority of the country) . . . a not unblemished Clarence Thomas was sworn into office and now serves on the nation's highest court. Given his present age and life expectancy, he may well hold that seat for almost twice as long as a large proportion of today's fifteen-to-twenty-five-year-old American black men will live. How could a man whose character and fitness for the job raised so many serious doubts on the part of so many thoughtful, serious people (aside from the political interests involved) during the confirmation process still go on to be given so much power? Is it just politics, we ask, or once again a reminder that women's lives and words do not count for very much?

Her ordeal over, Anita Hill returned to Norman, Oklahoma, her supporters hope, to put the events of her harrowing days in the glare of Washington, D.C.'s savage political arena behind her, and to resume the regular rhythms of her life. The faces, voices, and the ugly recriminations that from our television screens, radio speakers, and daily papers bombarded our senses during those eventful October days receded, and the bitter, open quarrel between these two well-matched, upwardly mobile, middle-class black people was no longer the focus of the entire country's attention. But some asked: could this really be the end?

One Told the Truth; the Other Lied

For a brief span of time the eyes and ears of the nation and the world had focused on the unrehearsed, riveting drama of two intelligent, successful African Americans locked in an acrimonious public struggle over their good names and the measure of their characters. Nor was this a simple difference of opinion. Few issues could have been more explosive; there were no possible loopholes to claim misunderstandings of the past they shared: one, we know, told the truth; the other lied; and the stakes in their confrontation seemed almost as high for both. By that time in the hearings, for Thomas, the results seemed likely to determine his defeat or success for the prize that represented the ultimate pinnacle of his career; for Hill, the outcome would be crucial to her ability to continue to build her own personal and professional future. Or we can reasonably assume that at least one of the principals saw it that way, and so did most onlookers.

Over the years, white Americans have grown accustomed to (and have even taken for granted) the appalling statistics on black-on-black crime among the least privileged of the group; never before had they had the chance to observe such a violent verbal disagreement of such personal dimensions between so articulate a woman and a man from among the privileged of the black race. Nor was this a private altercation inadvertently brought into public view, for in recent times sexual harassment in the workplace, regardless of the race or class or ages of the accusers or those accused, has become the single most crucial issue at the center of conflicts arising between women and men in every workplace in the country. When information on Anita Hill's allegations against Thomas and his denials first reached the media, she made clear that she would testify and openly reveal to the Senate and the nation the full nature of those allegations to "clear her name" of any suspicion that underhand motives prompted her to fabricate such awful charges against a man she knew, and on some levels, admired. So sure was she of her just position that she voluntarily took a polygraph test to prove her point. He, with a great display of arrogance, scorned the idea of submitting himself to such a test while he thundered and roared his denials, daring the white men chosen to decide on his fitness for the Court to deny him access to that seat.

Locker-Room Language

Once an employee of Clarence Thomas's, and now a tenured professor of law, called to testify before the Senate Judiciary Committee, Hill recollected (in male locker-room language so vivid it must have sometimes embarrassed the roomful of white men to whom she spoke) the lurid details of her claims of Thomas's breach of professional conduct and his abuse of her in the early 1980s. Even at the time of the hearings Hill was not a willing witness, and on her own would not have come forward with the charges. When the abuses occurred, she had coped with them privately as best she could, and then let them rest. That she agreed to make the allegations public when she did was testimony to her understanding of her civic duty in conjunction with her religious training and her sense of moral responsibility. Called upon as she had, even against her will, she could do no less than tell the truth of her experiences as she knew them, as sordid as that was, and as difficult as she must have found the telling. And when the public aspect of this trial by fire was over for her, to some, Anita Hill was a traitor to her race; or a liar; or at best a pawn of left-wing political activists with interests opposed to President George Bush's; to others she had struck the most powerful blow yet, after two decades of feminist struggle, against the sexual harassment of women in the workplace. The end could not be in the Senate hearing room in Washington, D.C.

While Europeans, much more accustomed to sexual scandals in their politics than we are, generally wondered what the fuss was all about, throughout the hearings the fever of American interest in the case and in its outcome ran extremely high. Reasons for this interest were varied. On one end, there were those who enjoyed the prurient titillation of the revelations—the legendary prowess of the black male, his out-of-control sexual appetite that for generations gave white mobs license to perpetrate enormous sufferings on the black community in the name of the "protection" of white womanhood from the "beast"; on the other end, there was a cross section of women in particular with deep concerns about the long-term effects of the exposé on Hill, and on the future of women's safety from sexual harassment in the places where they work. Many of these women, black and white, even felt that future prospects of women's willingness to speak out against this particular abuse—a recent phenomenon in which the few who speak are extremely reticent—rested on the outcome of Anita Hill's testimony.

Airing "Dirty Linen"

Between those poles of interest some blacks who supported the importance of Anita Hill's testimony in the hearings nevertheless worried about its implications. For example, there were concerns for the possible polarization effects such allegations could have on relationships between young black women and men, especially on those in the professional middle class. Other people expressed genuine anxieties about the social costs of such public "washing" of the race's "dirty linen." But the larger majority of African Americans, consisting mainly of the "folk" and working classes, but including intellectuals and professionals as well, oblivious to or rejecting the social significance of the racial-sexual politics in the drama they had witnessed, even believed that Hill's allegations were extraneous to the single goal they admitted: the confirmation of Clarence Thomas for a seat on the Supreme Court. In their minds Thomas's rise from the humblest of black beginnings to the nominee for the post made him deserving of that honor. In his favor some argued that in spite of his record to the contrary, once secure on the Court, he would remember his origins and support an agenda to benefit the least socially privileged. Early on, moderate and radical white feminists joined those who gave Hill their support, some unaware of the complexities embedded in a black woman's speaking out as she did against a black man. Nor, from the time that Hill spoke, were many people, white or black, women or men, neutral in their feelings on the merits of the opponents' positions: one either believed Anita Hill's clear and explicit accounts, or Clarence Thomas's passionate, boisterous denials of them. Those who supported Hill had not forgotten or counted for nothing that Thomas had been untruthful earlier in the hearings.

Ruin Her Reputation

But even now the calm that followed that storm is hardly a settling of the events of those charged days in October 1991. For who can forget the image of an articulate, impressively calm, self-possessed, courageous Anita Hill before the Senate committee, one who must have known that in order to save his nominee, the president would stop at nothing short of attempting to ruin her reputation; or the treatment she received at the hands of the white men she faced in the Senate hearing room; or that the majority of those who heard her testimony either did not believe or willed themselves not to believe her story; or when they acceded her belief, negated her courage and integrity by feeling that notwithstanding the nature of the circumstances, Clarence Thomas deserved to be confirmed. These aspects of the events cannot easily be put to rest. By the end, too, it was clear that Anita Hill, youngest daughter of a poor but loving family, a well-respected law professor, would never be the same as she had been before she went to Washington that fateful week. Never again, even in Norman, Oklahoma, will she be able to retreat from the larger-than-life public person she was that day in Washington into the anonymity of a small-town law professor. Having disturbed the routine dealings of the political power brokers in the nation's capital, and having achieved more than thousands (maybe millions) of feminist and feminist supporters have in twenty years of campaigns to raise the consciousness of all Americans on the issue of sexual harassment, her life will never again be as it was before she raised those allegations against Clarence Thomas. But, then, never again will she have to contemplate, in private rage or shame, the secret that she held within herself (revealing it partially only to her closest friends) for a decade of her life. She had recovered for herself the power that Clarence Thomas once tried to take from her, and even the Senate's contemptible treatment of her had not scarred her quiet dignity. . . .

In spite of the powerful politically backed efforts to ruin her reputation (how many black women have so directly adversely affected a presidential choice and themselves been such direct targets of the president's anger and will to destroy them?), with the exception of those with motives to discredit her, it was difficult for many of us who saw and heard Anita Hill before the Senate Judiciary Committee during those grueling hours to find her testimony other than convincing and sincere. She was impressive; and in appearance and demeanor she confirmed the words of others who knew her well and later spoke on her behalf. Politically conservative, deeply religious, by temperament repelled by the nature of the allegations she made, but a woman of strength and integrity willing to stand behind those allegations, however painful that stance was for her, she would have needed years of drama lessons to perfect her act that day had she been other than what she appeared to be.

Breaking the Silence

When she agreed to testify, Anita Hill was a woman confronted with the difficult choice of telling or not telling the

dirty details of what millions of women in this country suffer daily and are too afraid to dare tell. And in her telling,
millions of women identified with her, and understood per-
fectly well (even if some senators pretended they never did)
the power relations that kept her from pressing charges
against her harasser-employer at the time, and caused her
to promote an amicable relationship with him long after
she left his staff. During and after her testimony millions of
American women of all races dredged up long-buried memories of similar harassments in their pasts and felt in Anita
Hill's allegations the chance to finally exorcise uneasy
ghosts they attempted to bury long ago. And other women,
perhaps afraid to face compromises made with themselves
for survival when they did, denied themselves and her the
truth of the women's reality of which she spoke. But perhaps the greatest beneficiaries (besides herself) of Anita
Hill's publicly uttering her allegations of sexual harassment
against Clarence Thomas, a black man (one with influence
and power), are the millions of black women for whom her
action represented a further breaking of the bonds of generations of black women's silence on and denial of their differences with black men, because of gender issues, and
their right to be full human beings despite the conflicts of
race and sex. For in all of their lives in America, whatever
the issue, black women have felt torn between the loyalties
that bind them to race on one hand, and sex on the other.
Choosing one or the other, of course, means taking sides
against the self, yet they have almost always chosen race
over the other: a sacrifice of their self-hood as women and
of full humanity, in favor of the race. . . .

A Model of Achievement

The majority of black people who supported Clarence
Thomas's nomination (before and after Anita Hill's allegations became public) did so because of his race, which for
them far outweighed other considerations. Although
Thomas had spent most of his forty-three years distancing
himself from his lowly background, they identified with

him on that basis. As the nominee for the Court, to them he symbolized the ultimate in black triumph over hundreds of years of racial oppression. For decades to come, his name will be held up as a model of achievement for countless young black boys and girls in his native Georgia and in places far and wide across this country. This identification with and support for Thomas is not difficult to understand, for it comes directly out of the long history of the racial oppression of Africans and African Americans in this country, beginning with slavery, passing through the postbellum years of legal segregation and other race-restricting social codes, and continuing in the present forms of discrimination that still deny millions of black people equal access to the promise of America. Buried deep in the collective black psyche, but never outside of easy recollection, is the knowledge that underlying racial oppression in this country are long-held white theories of the inherent inferiority of people of African descent. For numbers of black people, every major success by any black person puts a nail in the coffin of those theories and further advances the group. The Thomas nomination to the Court was, for them, another success for the race.

"Treason Against the Race"

Consequently, for many black people, Anita Hill's speaking out against Clarence Thomas as she did, even in telling the truth, was an act of much larger dimensions than possibly undermining the credibility and fitness of the then-judge for the job to which he aspired. In the first place, any allegations she could make that cast doubt on the wisdom or rightness of the nomination of Judge Thomas to the Supreme Court would violate the racial taboo of revealing "family affairs" to the white world. But more serious than what might be ascertained an "inappropriate airing of dirty linen," in exposing a situation that called into question the sexual conduct of a black man, to those minds, Anita Hill committed treason against the race. This was the most serious infraction she could make against the understood inviolability of race loyalty. This loyalty espouses that the oppression that black men have suffered and continue to suffer at the hands of the white world entitles them to the unqualified support of black women, even to their self-denial. Interestingly, there are no circumstances that require such a sacrifice of black men.

In this light, for most African Americans the stand-off between Anita Hill and Clarence Thomas was a matter of grave concern that had deep roots in the troubled history of the group. In fact, black men have long contended that black women often work against the best interests of the race, and of its men in particular, in their relationships with white liberal men and feminists especially. While it is true that the women have been more mobile than the men, achieve social successes in larger numbers, and have more stable records of employment (although they have lower-status jobs and earn less than black men), that has partly been true because black women have more singlemind-edly—not only for themselves but for all black people—pursued survival, and always were willing to do necessary work, however menial—work that white women and men have not wanted to do—to keep themselves and others alive. For example, seldom, no matter how difficult the circumstances of their lives, do black women leave their children to the mercy of the world; the absent father is both stereotype and, too often, reality in the black community. In addition, black women never spend the psychic energy doubting their womanhood that black men do in struggling to recover their manhood lost to slavery and to more contemporary black oppressions. . . .

High-Tech Lynching

[During testimony Thomas] pointed his finger, raised a thunderous voice to the Senate committee, and challenged the fourteen white men in that chamber to use Anita Hill's testimony to deny his confirmation. In calling the proceedings a "high-tech lynching," a vulgar display of temper or loss of self-control, he provoked and shocked his listeners, even some of his supporters. If the committee did not recommend his confirmation, regardless of sentiments entertained prior to the latter portion of the hearings, he would hold Anita Hill's testimony and white male racial discrimination responsible for his defeat. Thus, Clarence Thomas pointedly accused his former aide of that old bugaboo: black women's complicity with white men against black men. At the same time, since lynching is always (although erroneously) associated with race and sex, Thomas's evocation of the single most emotional issue at the heart of the black and white community's relationship further inscribed his determined use of racial-sexual politics to gain his ends.

Rodney King and the Los Angeles Riots

The Staff of the *Los Angeles Times*

Issues of racial discrimination exploded onto American television screens in March 1991 when CNN began broadcasting a video every thirty minutes of an African American man named Rodney King being beaten and kicked by a half dozen Los Angeles police officers who also yelled racial epithets at the prone man. In this selection, the staff of the *Los Angeles Times* documents the gulf between the races and how it widened into a huge chasm on April 29, 1992, when the four officers involved in the beating were acquitted of any wrongdoing. What followed was four days of burning, looting, rioting, and murder in Los Angeles that left fifty-four dead, caused $1 billion in property damage, and destroyed at least twenty-five thousand jobs. In the biggest riot in American history, rioters destroyed over thirty-eight hundred buildings and vandalized, looted, and burned another ten thousand.

Surrounded by a clutch of police officers in the glare of patrol car headlights, a large man rises from the ground and lurches in the direction of a baton-wielding cop. The officer swings once, catching the man in the upper body and dropping him face-first to the pavement. Then he steps

---

forward to hammer the man again and again.

Another officer joins the fray, swinging his own metal baton and repeatedly kicking the man writhing on the ground. A third officer enters the semicircle of blue uniforms and administers what appears to be yet another kick. Seconds creep like hours as the batons continue to swing, 56 times in all.

"Oh, my God, they're beating him to death!" a horrified woman wails from her balcony in a nearby apartment building. "What are they going to do, kill him?"

Her cry isn't registered by the hand-held video camera used by plumber George Holliday to capture the assault on tape, but millions of television viewers who watch the images repeatedly in coming weeks will share the thought.

Once seen, the TV footage of the beating of Rodney King is difficult to forget. The violence is harsh, brutal, savage. Almost as chilling is what the camera doesn't capture—the message that one of the baton-swinging officers, Laurence M. Powell, sent to another officer minutes before the episode in Lake View Terrace. The words seem to confirm the community's most serious qualms about its Police Department's worst members. Before confronting King, Powell had likened a black family's domestic dispute to "Gorillas in the Mist." After King was subdued, some witnesses said the arresting officers bragged of their violence and taunted their victim.

Dr. Edmund Chein, one of five emergency room physicians who tended to King immediately after the beating, said the officers' baton strokes were so violent they literally knocked the fillings out of some of King's teeth. One of King's eye sockets was shattered, a cheekbone was fractured, a leg broken. His flesh was bruised by the repeated blows. A concussion and painful facial nerve damage complicated his other injuries.

Two Dozen Law Officers

The incident began soon after midnight, March 3, 1991, when King, a 25-year-old high school dropout and part-time Dodger Stadium groundskeeper from Altadena, passed a California Highway Patrol car on the Foothill Freeway in Sun Valley. King was out with a couple of friends for a night of driving, talking and drinking. The CHP cruiser pulled behind his white 1988 Hyundai and flashed its red lights. King, who was on parole for a second-degree robbery conviction, panicked and sped up. After he exited the freeway, LAPD units joined the chase.

When King finally did stop, near a large apartment complex, more than two dozen law enforcement officers—21 from the LAPD, four from the CHP and two from the Los Angeles Unified School District—converged on his car. Police later said that King, following an officer's orders, emerged from his Hyundai and lay on the ground. Powell sought to handcuff the prone man, police said, but King flung Powell and other officers away.

"That's when the fight started," said Richard Talkington, the LAPD traffic detective who initially investigated the incident.

Most witnesses in the apartment building said King was calm, complying with the officers' orders to get out of the car and lie on the ground. They said police hit him in the chest with a Taser stun gun as he lay on his back, then clubbed him without provocation. One CHP officer at the scene said that King appeared amused by the small army of officers, not combative. His most threatening gesture, she said, was to grab his buttocks while parading in front of them. She thought he was drunk but not dangerous.

Los Angeles police, however, insisted that King *was* dangerous. That he reached in a pocket, as if he were armed, when he stepped from his car. That he ignored orders to lie still on the ground. That he seemed to be on PCP, a powerful drug that can spur reckless aggression in people—though tests found no evidence of the drug in King's system.

King himself had a fuzzy memory of the event. He conceded that he and his friends had been drinking malt liquor and that he had run from the CHP to try to dodge a ticket. But he said he never would have been fool enough to resist arrest, especially while surrounded by so many armed officers. . . .

Reaction to the tape was swift and sharp. The grainy video images of police beating a prone and pleading man were powerful enough to yank the nation's attention from the grainy video images of guided missiles smashing Iraq in the just-concluded Gulf War.

Mayor Tom Bradley, himself a former LAPD officer, was "shocked and outraged" and promised a swift prosecution of the officers involved. "This is something which we cannot and will not tolerate," he said. Even other police professionals were unnerved by the ferocity of the beating. Dallas Police Chief William Rathburn, a former assistant chief of the LAPD, called it "gross criminal misconduct." LAPD Officer Tom Sullivan, expressing the shame and anger of many cops, said, "This isn't just a case of excessive force. It's a case of mass stupidity."

Regular citizens started giving cops dirty looks, making obscene gestures. And this was in the Valley, on the Westside, where police thought they could count on support. A *Los Angeles Times* Poll in the week after the beating found that 92% of Angelenos believed the police used excessive force against King. Two-thirds thought police brutality was common. . . .

The Worst Riots Ever

In South Los Angeles, anger had exploded into action [when the officers accused of beating King were found not guilty]. When police officers confronted a crowd at 71st Street and Normandie Avenue, people hurled rocks and bottles. A block away, at Florence Avenue and Normandie, about 200 people milled, many with raised fists. They hurled chunks of pavement at passing cars. Then, people mobbed cars, dragging light-skinned motorists into the street, robbing and beating them.

The worst riots of the century had begun.

Into the storm rumbled Reginald Denny, the truck driver, hauling 27 tons of sand toward an Inglewood cement-mixing plant. At about 6:30 P.M., his 18-wheeler rolled into the intersection. Rocks and bottles whizzed past. Overturned trash cans littered the street. As Denny slowed down, several black men surrounded the rig. One yanked open the truck door and pulled Denny from his cab. At least two others beat him in the head and kicked him, knocking him to the ground. After kicking him, one man raised his hands in triumph. As Denny tried to move, another man bashed his skull with a fire extinguisher from the truck.

The attack was broadcast live on TV.

Watching from his home, T.J. Murphy, a 30-year-old, black, unemployed aerospace engineer, and his friend, Tee

Burning Korean Businesses

Sixty percent of the buildings damaged in the Los Angeles riots belonged to Korean-American merchants whose relationships with their black customers had been tense for some time. In 1991 the wife of a Korean grocer shot a black teenager named Latasha Harlins in the back after the grocer accused her of stealing a bottle of orange juice. The incident was caught on videotape by the store's security camera and was replayed on the news hundreds of times. The grocer received a lenient sentence of probation by a white judge.

[A merchant named] Kang, a college-educated Korean American . . . in his early forties, who gave a sustained "structural" (his word) analysis—"Koreans were doing the wrong businesses in the wrong place at the wrong time"—offered a powerful indictment of the U.S. government's suppression of the riots: "Basically, the orders were to draw a line, to cordon off the affluent neighborhoods, and to tell the looters, 'OK, you play here in Koreatown and South Central.' It was a topsy-turvy time and police orders were all backwards, inside-out, and upside down—Gates [Los Angeles Chief of Police] is not a human being, he's a bastard. The police, well they came out 'big' when it was safe, and

Barnett, 28, were appalled. "Somebody's got to get that guy out of there," they said to each other. They headed for the nearby intersection, never thinking the rescue might fall to them. But the police were nowhere to be seen. The injured man—his face awash in blood and his eyes swollen shut—had somehow managed to get back behind the wheel and was making his getaway an inch at a time.

A woman, a nutrition consultant on her way home from work, had hoisted herself onto the side of the truck cab and was shouting steering instructions to Denny. Then she climbed inside to console Denny as a black-clad young man

retreated in the face of real danger."

Korean American businesses were thus in the "looter's playground," abandoned by the police. Chae, the owner of a swap meet building that burned to the ground during the riots, stands to lose $600,000 if he cannot "go back in." He commented that "the whole thing is a man-made disaster, isn't it?" He continued, "I mean, didn't everyone know it was going to happen, see it coming?" He was active in a grassroots movement of Korean Americans who aimed to sue the city of Los Angeles for not protecting them during the riots. For Chae and others, the covenant had been broken. He also noted, "It just happened to be Koreans who were there at that time; it's the city's fault." The shop owner So Chung told *Village Voice* reporters that there were conscious decisions involved in the betrayal of Koreatown. "Daryl Gates wanted the blacks to let out their outburst toward the Koreans . . . because he knew that the blacks didn't feel very good toward the Koreans. I do believe there must have been some conscious politics, because [the police] just weren't there." A shop owner suggested that the media showed the looters "how easy it was to loot, calling out the looters; it was a real propellant, as if to say— don't worry, there are no police here."

Nancy Abelmann and John Lie, *Blue Dreams: Korean Americans and the Los Angeles Riots*. Cambridge, MA: Harvard University Press, 1995.

took over the driving. The new driver was unable to see through the shattered windshield, so Murphy clung to the side of the truck and guided him. "You're going to make it," the consultant kept telling Denny, "You're going to be OK."

As the driver tried desperately to speed up the heavy rig, Barnett drove in front of the truck, putting on her hazard lights to try to clear the way. After a trip that seemed to take hours, the rig lurched into the driveway at Daniel Freeman Memorial Hospital. Denny went into a convulsion, spitting up blood. One minute longer, a paramedic said, and the 36-year-old father wouldn't have made it.

Where Are the Police?

In the Crenshaw District, Holly Echols was one of many glued to the television. A 33-year-old media relations manager who is black, she lived with her 9-year-old daughter, Aja. She knew there would be a bad reaction to the verdicts. She had found herself on a three-way call with her sister and her mother. Her mother had cried; none of them could believe the verdicts. "It's going to be worse than [the riots of] '65," Echols' mother predicted. "There's going to be trouble tonight."

By that time, people were honking their horns in protest as they drove up and down Crenshaw Boulevard, just two blocks away. Echols could hear shooting. She turned out the lights. On the television screen, the violence was escalating; people were being yanked from their cars.

"Where are the police? Where the hell are the police? I don't believe this!" she screamed at the television. ". . . This is not tape, this is live! And there are no police. There's no ambulance. There's no firemen. What the hell is going on?"

Television anchors, reporters and viewers across the country asked the same question as they watched mobs drag motorists from their cars—beating them to a pulp without any sign of police.

The police, it would turn out, had already come and gone. Earlier, many officers of the 77th Street Division had tried and failed to stop the growing violence. Severely outnumbered, a field commander had ordered his troops to withdraw. They had retreated to a secure, cinder-block-walled bus terminal at 54th Street and Arlington Avenue—an emergency police command center 30 blocks from where Reginald Denny lay.

At about 4:30 P.M., Kris Owen and partner Steve Zaby had heard the first disturbance call: Six black men were smashing car windows with baseball bats. Nearing Florence and 71st, Owen's cruiser was hit by a volley of bricks and rocks. Other officers were attending an injured white driver who had been pulled from his Volvo. Over his portable radio, Owen heard a family had been attacked and beaten in their car near Florence and Normandie. He and Zaby raced to the scene and found a terrified Latino couple with a 1-year-old child. Their faces were bloody, cut by broken glass. Owen and Zaby hustled the family back to the squad car and drove them to the hospital. . . .

Once the sun had set, looting and burning began in earnest. One of the first targets was Tom's Liquor and Deli at Florence and Normandie. The first fire call came in at 7:45 P.M. as rampaging rioters began torching buildings in South Los Angeles. . . .

A Poverty Riot

Throughout South Los Angeles, poor Latino residents joined their black neighbors in looting the hundreds of liquor stores and discount clothing outlets that lined Florence, Figueroa, Slauson and other thoroughfares. At the corner of Slauson and Vermont, hundreds of people ransacked the Indoor Swap Meet. Pregnant women emerged carrying boxes of diapers and baby food. It was clear: The protest over police abuse had become a poverty riot. Latino residents who had barely heard of Rodney King helped bend back iron security bars so they could loot at will.

Myung Lee had fled her doughnut shop early. "Get out!" the voice on the telephone had said. It was another Korean merchant several blocks east, at Florence and Normandie. William Hong had fled his liquor store, too. In the confusing overlay of TV pictures—the cameras shifted from South Los Angeles to police headquarters to Compton, tracking an ever-widening circle of fiery destruction—Lee at home in North Hollywood and Hong at home in Simi Valley found it impossible to tell whether their stores had survived.

Leticia, the unemployed illegal immigrant from Mexico City, had been caught in traffic during the first outburst of rioting and had rushed to her apartment, next to Hong's liquor store. She called her roommate, Anna, at work. Get back here! she insisted. By the time Anna made it home, people were looting Hong's store. They were breaking the windows in the doughnut shop, busting into the video store where Leticia had rented a tape hours before. Most of the women in the apartment building joined in. Why not? they figured. Everyone else was doing it. Leticia went inside Hong's store. It was muddy and slippery. Everybody was pushing and shoving. Many of the apartment residents took milk, butter and other food. Leticia, who has no children, did not.

"We told ourselves we were taking things because we were needy. Because we were poor. But when we got home and saw what we had taken, there was only beer," she said. She drank so much "free" beer she got drunk and went to sleep.

Anna locked herself inside the apartment until a neighbor came to warn them that a group of black men—led by a neighbor they knew only as Mike—was about to torch Hong's liquor store and the other Asian-owned storefronts. They held crude torches made of sticks. "They were thinking of every excuse they could to burn the building," Anna said later. "'This Korean cheated us.' 'This other Korean was mean to us.'" Anna pleaded with them not to burn the building: "Go somewhere else. You'll burn my house down. There's families with children living next door." Mike knew Anna; she was cool. He agreed not to torch Hong's store. The mob set fire to a grocery across the street instead. . . .

"Total Chaos"

By 9 P.M., normal life throughout Los Angeles had been derailed. Every police officer in the city had been ordered to report for duty. Public and parochial schools were being shut down in a 30-square-mile area. Children were to stay at home, indoors. Dozens of bus lines in South Los Angeles were being halted. With the rioting spreading to Inglewood, Mayor Bradley declared a local state of emergency. Minutes later, at Bradley's request, Gov. Wilson ordered the National Guard to activate 2,000 reserve soldiers.

The demonstration at police headquarters had turned violent. Protesters set fire to a kiosk, so the police line moved to break up the crowd. People turned and ran, fanning out through the area, vandalizing other buildings, smashing cars and hurtling newspaper boxes through plate-glass windows. They stopped off at City Hall, then the Los Angeles Times building, where they broke out nearly every first-floor window, pelted third-floor newsroom windows with concrete chunks and trashed some first-floor offices. Others headed for the Hollywood Freeway, torching palm trees. As rioters lunged out into the freeway traffic, a few panicked drivers turned and fled against oncoming cars.

At 9:05 P.M., the California Highway Patrol closed many freeway exit ramps on the Harbor Freeway in hopes of keeping unsuspecting motorists from wandering into the path of violence. At Los Angeles International Airport, the Federal Aviation Administration shifted the landing pattern of approaching jetliners after the police reported that one of their helicopters had been fired upon. Suddenly, it seemed, everyone had guns. Dozens of pawnshops and other businesses stocked with firearms were systematically looted during the first few hours of the unrest, putting thousands of guns onto the streets. On South Western Avenue, suspected gang members broke into the Western Surplus store and carted off as many as 1,700 guns, plus ammunition. Outside the riot-damaged areas, fearful residents crowded into gun stores, clamoring for firearms. They bought the only ones immediately available—surplus rifles from World War II.

By late Wednesday, authorities would report that at least 10 people had been killed, nine of them shooting victims.

O.J. Simpson and "the Trial of the Century"

Gilbert Geis and Leigh B. Bienen

In this selection Gilbert Geis, professor emeritus in the department of criminology, law, and society at the University of California, Irvine, and Leigh B. Bienen, a senior lecturer at Northwestern University School of Law, explore the issues behind the O.J. Simpson murder trial. Geis and Bienen discuss police misconduct, interracial marriage, spousal abuse, celebrity in America, and media conspiracy against black men. What became known as "the Trial of the Century" began when Nicole Brown, the former wife of football hero and media spokesman O.J. Simpson, was found stabbed to death along with a friend, Ron Goldman. For three years the murders and subsequent arrest and trial of Simpson dominated newspaper headlines and dozens of television talk and news shows, making celebrities of the lawyers and judges involved in the case. When Simpson was found not guilty in spite of positive DNA evidence, 85 percent of African Americans polled agreed with the verdict and 80 percent thought the jury was fair. By contrast, only 32 percent of whites agreed with the verdict, and only 50 percent thought the jury was "fair and impartial."

This is likely what happened:

Sometime during the hour after ten o'clock on the evening of June 12, 1994, a lone person came through the back entrance of a Spanish-style, four-bedroom condominium on Bundy Drive in the upscale Los Angeles suburb of Brentwood. In the small, almost caged area near the front gate, the intruder savagely slashed a woman, virtually severing her neck from her body, apparently after she had been rendered unconscious. . . . In the same entryway, the killer stabbed a man to death, inflicting at least thirty wounds.

Determination of the order in which the two victims were slashed to death was based on the fact that there was no blood on the female's bare feet, while plentiful blood was present on the soles of the man's white shoes.

The woman, dressed in a black halter sundress, was thirty-five-year-old Nicole Brown Simpson, the recently divorced wife of O.J. (for Orenthal James) Simpson, a one-time football superstar and later a media notable. The couple had two children, both of whom were asleep in an upstairs bedroom in the condominium. The dead man, dressed in jeans, was twenty-five-year-old Ronald Goldman, a social acquaintance of Ms. Simpson. Goldman was a waiter at the Mezzaluna restaurant, where Ms. Simpson and her family had eaten earlier that evening. He was returning the gold-rimmed prescription sunglasses that Ms. Simpson's mother had dropped on the curb while getting into her car in front of the restaurant. A person with a mordant sense of humor later would place signs outside the Mezzaluna reading, "Don't forget your sunglasses."

At ten minutes after midnight the following morning—more than three hours after they had been slain—the bodies of Nicole Simpson and Goldman were discovered by a neighbor who had been led to the site by a howling brown-and-white Akita, a big dog that was obviously distraught. The dog, which belonged to Nicole Simpson, had blood on its belly, paws, and legs.

Few of the foregoing "facts" have gone undisputed,

however. Some maintain that the killer's entry was from the front of the condominium. Others believe that Nicole Simpson, learning of the loss of the eyeglasses from her mother, requested Goldman to deliver them and was planning a sexual interlude with him—or perhaps with someone else. Her erotic invitations characteristically involved the lighting of candles in her residence, as she had done this evening. There are those who believe that there was more than one killer, and some who believe that drug dealing retaliation was central to the murders.

A Trash Novel Come to Life

The savage killing of Nicole Simpson and Ronald Goldman and the subsequent arrest and trial of her former husband unleashed a cascade of events that preoccupied much of America for the following three years. Fiery disputes arose about the not-guilty verdict and the importance of the racial composition of the jury, which was made up of eight black and two white women and one black and one Latino man, though the initial pool from which it was selected was 40 percent white, 28 percent African American, 17 percent Hispanic, and 15 percent Asian. . . .

Commentators . . . pointed to what they saw as incompetence, perjury, and perhaps conspiratorial actions by detectives in the Los Angeles Police Department, to blatant racism in their ranks, to the considerable lawyering inadequacies of the prosecution team, and to questionable tactics by the defense lawyers. Dominick Dunne, a writer who was favored with a reserved seat at the proceedings, summarized events this way:

> The Simpson case is like a great trash novel come to life, a mammoth fireworks display of interracial marriage, love, lust, lies, hate, fame, wealth, beauty, obsession, spousal abuse, stalking, broken-hearted children, the bloodiest of bloody knife-slashing homicides and all the justice money can buy.

Questions surfaced about whether television ought to be

permitted in courtrooms, whether juries should be sequestered, and whether unanimous verdicts should be required in order to convict in a criminal trial.

The price of "justice" in the Simpson criminal case mounted to an estimated $6 million expenditure by the defendant and $9 million by the prosecution, of which $2.6 million went for housing, feeding, and other expenses associated with jury sequestration.

O.J. Simpson was the obvious initial suspect, and when he later was tried for the murders he became the most famous person ever prosecuted for homicide in the annals of American criminal justice, with the possible exception of [18th-century vice-president] Aaron Burr. As a football hero at the University of Southern California, Simpson won the Heisman trophy, awarded each year to the athlete deemed to be the outstanding football player in the nation. Subsequently, he was a running back for nine years with the Buffalo Bills and two with the San Francisco '49ers in the National Football League. His stellar athletic performances earned him a spot in the National Football Hall of Fame after his retirement. In the following years, Simpson appeared in widely seen Hertz commercials, served as a commentator on professional football games, and acted in several easily forgotten motion pictures.

"He's Going to Kill Me"

Simpson's first marriage to his high school sweetheart, Marguerite Whitley, produced two children. He met Nicole, eleven years younger than he, when she was an eighteen-year-old waitress at the Daisy, a fancy Beverly Hills nightclub. They dated for a year, then lived together for six more before their marriage in 1985. The marital relationship turned tumultuous, with several raw incidents of domestic violence, usually associated with drinking, that resulted in calls to the police. Jurors heard Nicole's terrified scream, "He's going to kill me," recorded when she called a police dispatcher on New Year's Day 1989. The Simpsons would separate, then reconcile, usually on Nicole's initiative, and then split again. They were divorced in 1992; Nicole received a sizable settlement and child support payments of $10,000 a month. In April 1993 Nicole was imploring Simpson to consider reuniting the family, writing that she loved him deeply. Along with her letter she sent videos showing their marriage ceremony and the birth of their children. But three weeks before she was killed, Nicole appeared to have emotionally distanced herself from Simpson.

Along with her will, Simpson's former wife had left a picture of herself in her safe deposit box showing her face severely abraded and bruised, the result of a dispute between them. For some, the only worthwhile thing to emerge from the trial was a growing public concern with domestic violence—or "domestic discord," as the defense sought to label it in order to de-escalate the emotions engendered by terms such as "spousal abuse" and "wife battering." Defense attorneys debated introducing evidence that very few episodes of domestic violence lead to murder, but they decided that it was best to downplay the entire issue. During the year following the trial, reports to police of domestic violence increased by sixty percent in Los Angeles; the family of Simpson's slain ex-wife established the Nicole Brown Simpson Charitable Foundation for Battered Women to fight domestic violence, naming Nicole's father president and her three sisters to the board of directors.

Nicole was a self-described party animal, part of a group of fast livers who played a lot, often dancing at nightspots until the early hours of the morning. As was her husband, she was sexually promiscuous. . . . She apparently did not have a sexual relationship with Goldman, though he had been seen driving her $90,000 white Ferrari Mondiale convertible (with the personalized license plate L84AD8—late for a date). Goldman and Ms. Simpson had met casually at dances and at The Gym, a trendy Brentwood fitness center and health club. He had filed for bankruptcy in 1992, listing debts of about $12,000. In a typical tactic of slander by innuendo, defense attorney Robert Shapiro would write after the trial that "our investigation was to discover much information about Nicole that was of an intimate and possibly inflammatory nature. It was relevant to the case and we chose not to use it as part of the defense. I choose not to use it now."

Differences in Black and White

The defense had learned from simulated jury tests that black women harbored a biting dislike of Nicole Simpson—a white woman they saw as milking the money of a famous black man and living an irresponsible life of luxury. The black female jurors also were hostile to prosecutor Marcia Clark, offering credence to the observation of the novelist Toni Morrison, a Nobel Prize–winner, that black women are very different from white women, but that black and white men are much the same.

During the trial, the defense dealt with Nicole's behavior and character with care, making certain that they did not too meanly blacken the reputation of a victim when nothing that she had done could possibly exculpate her murderer from legal guilt. But they pointed out that Simpson had supported her in grand scale, putting a paid-for half-million-dollar house in San Francisco in her name, and sending two of her sisters to college until each in turn dropped out. . . . Simpson also had secured the Hertz franchise at the upscale Ritz-Carlton Hotel in Orange County for Nicole's father and had directed considerable business to her mother's travel agency.

Simpson had flown to Chicago for a business meeting on a late-night flight the evening that Nicole was killed. When he returned home the following day, he was interrogated at police headquarters for thirty-two minutes by homicide detectives, who primarily focused on the nasty cut that he had on his right hand. Simpson claimed at first that he did not know how he had gotten the injury, then suggested that it probably was the result of his reaching into his Bronco when he was hurriedly preparing to leave for Chicago. The wound had reopened, he maintained, when he broke a glass during the period of anguish in his hotel room after he had been told of the murder of his ex-wife. Details of the police interrogation, stunningly short and totally inept in regard to asking tough follow-up questions, would not be introduced into the trial. The prosecution presumably preferred not to have the jury hear Simpson's proclamations of innocence, and the defense wanted to avoid any focus on the inconsistent stories about the source of Simpson's cut hand.

The Famous Ride

When a warrant for Simpson's arrest was issued, his lawyer said that he would turn himself in at police headquarters. Instead, Simpson took off in the early afternoon with his close friend, A.C. (Al) Cowlings, Jr., in Cowlings's white Bronco. After the car was spotted by another motorist at 6:20 in the evening in nearby Orange County, where Nicole's family lived, it was followed by a phalanx of a dozen police cars, its every move filmed by news reporters from helicopters as it slowly wove its way along sixty miles of southern California freeways before going to Simpson's Brentwood home.

Media accounts, labeling this the most famous ride on American shores since Paul Revere's, reported that ninety-five million Americans watched the convoy. Simpson had left behind a long note, saturated with misspellings and full of self-pity and self-righteousness. He insisted on his innocence and indicated rather clearly that he intended to commit suicide. The letter ended: "Don't feel sorry for me. I've had a great life. Great friends. Please think of the real OJ and not this lost person. Thanks for making my life special. I hope I helped yours." There also were some indications that Simpson might have intended to flee the country. The destination seemed to be Mexico, until the car was spotted. In the car were his passport, $8,750 in cash and traveler's checks, and a loaded gun. There also was a disguise, a false goatee and mustache, bought two weeks before the murder at the Cinema Secrets Beauty Shop in Burbank. Neither the note nor the presumed attempted escape would be placed before the jury.

An Open-and-Shut Case?

For some persons, the crucial miscalculation by the district attorney's office was made well before the first trial witness was called. It involved the decision to try the case in downtown Los Angeles rather than in Santa Monica, the court that typically assumes jurisdiction over crimes that occur in its vicinity. In Los Angeles, juries are recruited among persons who live within a twenty-mile radius of each courthouse. If the trial had been held in Santa Monica, the odds are that the jury would have had a majority of white members rather than racial and ethnic minorities. Numerous explanations would be offered for the venue change, including the central location of the downtown courthouse and its ability to more readily accommodate the media crush. There also was expressed concern about the recent earthquake damage suffered by the Santa Monica courthouse.

Some people believe that the downtown site was selected to avoid any implication that the jury might be stacked against Simpson. Earlier, a jury of white persons in suburban Simi Valley had acquitted police officers of the severe beating of a black man, Rodney King, despite a videotape that vividly showed what they had done to him. Street rioting erupted in the wake of that jury decision, an outcome the authorities wanted to avoid in the Simpson case. Others say that the choice was ruled by the arrogance of the district attorney, who was determined to be closely involved in dictating prosecution tactics and who believed that he had an open-and-shut case against Simpson. Marcia Clark, who would prosecute the case, reassured one skeptic that the state "would do equally well in L.A." and "would have a clear-cut guilty verdict regardless of where O.J. was tried." Bill Hodgman, Clark's superior until illness early in the case forced him into a background role, has offered an even simpler explanation for the case's not being tried in Santa Monica: "Nobody even thought about it at the time."

The prosecution also forfeited another strategic advantage when it decided not to seek the death penalty, though the twin killings would have permitted it to do so. This decision undoubtedly was based on the fact that Simpson did not match the stereotype of a "real" criminal, and the prosecution feared alienating jurors who might have believed a death penalty demand was too merciless. But "death-qualified" jurors, it is well known, tend to convict a defendant more readily than panels whose members may not be willing to inflict capital punishment.

"One Hundred Percent Not Guilty"

The trial of O.J. Simpson on the double-murder charge began on July 22, 1994, with the defendant answering the judge's request "How do you plead?" with "Absolutely one hundred percent not guilty, Your Honor." The trial would last until October 2, 1995, more than a year and two months later. Simpson spent 473 days in jail before the jury rendered its verdict. The prosecution called seventy-eight witnesses; the defense, with nine attorneys, summoned seventy-two witnesses. The original jury panel melted down as one after another of its members was dismissed for cause or themselves asked to be relieved. During the trial, the jury was sequestered for 266 days—housed in the Inter-Continental Hotel and permitted only weekend visits from family members. The sequestration produced an esprit de corps within the group, a climate that undoubtedly played into the rapid return of a verdict.

Two very distinct trials of O.J. Simpson were taking place. One was held in the courtroom, the other in the newspapers and, particularly, on television, with several major channels broadcasting everything that took place during the court sessions. What the cameras chose to focus on was what the viewing public saw: particular people's expressions, the judge's activities, a restless bailiff. These often were different images from those that imprinted themselves on the jurors' minds.

Besides, jurors heard only segments of what the public learned. Television showed arguments between the lawyers while the jury had been removed from the courtroom. Court intermissions and recesses were filled by a host of commentators and lawyers ("talking heads") who offered opinions about what had gone on. These people typically felt compelled to turn each day into a sporting contest, asking: "Who won?" "Who does this benefit?" "Who is ahead?" Notable was the remark by juror Marsha Rubin-Jackson when interviewed on NBC's *Dateline* after the trial. "I don't want to get this wrong," she said, "because I am standing by my verdict, but based on what I've heard since I've been out [of the courtroom], I would have to vote guilty."

CHAPTER 5

Pop Goes the Culture

AMERICA'S DECADES

Nonstop Talk

Howard Kurtz

The 1990s saw the rise of the "twenty-four-hour news cycle" in which dozens of news, entertainment, and talk shows competed with each other to instantly gather, dissect, and analyze news. In this selection journalist Howard Kurtz contends that the days of fact checking and attempting to balance viewpoints were quickly abandoned in order to keep up with this fast-paced news cycle. As the 1990s drew to a close, important issues that affected all Americans were argued on shows where the panel of guests yelling at each other were commonly compared to food fights.

Kurtz is a reporter for the *Washington Post*, a winner of *American Journalism Review*'s best book award, and a journalist whose work has appeared in the *New Republic*, *New York* magazine, and others.

America is awash in talk. Loud talk. Angry talk. Conspiratorial talk. Raunchy talk, smug talk, self-serving talk, funny talk, rumor-mongering talk. A cacophony of chat fills the airwaves from coast to coast, from dawn to dusk and beyond, all talk all the time.

The richest and most prominent talkers include a wide assortment of pundits, commentators, experts, hacks, and hucksters, some of them cloaked in the thinnest journalistic garb. They analyze, interpret, elucidate, expound, pontificate, and predict, an unprecedented barrage of blather and bluster that has dramatically ratcheted up the noise level of political debate.

But many of the talkers are ordinary Americans, aggrieved, frustrated, flooding the switchboards of television and radio studios to register their dissent. Gradually, with little warning, this has produced a high-decibel revolution in the way we communicate with each other and with our leaders. We have become a talk show nation, pulsating with opinions that are channeled through hosts and reverberate through the vast echo chamber of the airwaves.

The Old Media—the big newspapers, magazines, and network newscasts—still cling to some vestige of objectivity, the traditional notion that information must be checked and verified and balanced with opposing views before it can be disseminated to the public. But the talk shows revel in their one-sided pugnacity, spreading wild theories, delicious gossip, and angry denunciations with gleeful abandon. Anyone can say anything at any time with little fear of contradiction. It is raw, it is real, and it is immensely popular. The gatekeepers of the elite media have been cast aside and the floodgates thrown open.

Extremism in Pursuit of Ratings

There is, however, a price to be paid for this unending marathon of talk. As the talk show culture has exploded, the national conversation has been coarsened, cheapened, reduced to name-calling and finger-pointing and bumper-sticker sloganeering. Television has little time for context, subtlety, or caveats. Seat-of-the-pants judgments—up or down, yes or no, who won and who lost and who committed the outrage of the week—have become a driving force behind the shrill and often mean-spirited politics of the 1990s.

Outlandish opinion-mongers on the left and right tend to drown out everyone else. Extremism in the pursuit of ratings is no vice. The middle ground, the sensible center, is dismissed as too squishy, too dull, too likely to send the audience channel surfing. Rhetoric heats up and consensus melts away. There was a time when "Jane, you ignorant slut!" was a great late-night gag; now the parody cuts uncomfortably close to reality. The whole point of the talk show business is not so much to persuade as to posture, to slam-dunk opponents and to build audience share.

Let's face it: Talk is cheap. The armchair warriors defuse world crises, wipe out budget deficits, and solve the welfare mess, all before the commercial break: And it's all make-believe. They don't have to build coalitions or crunch numbers or live with the consequences of their errors. If they screw up, there's always next week's show to test-drive new theories.

News Cycle on Fast Forward

With so many talkers talking around the clock, the news cycle is permanently stuck on fast-forward. Events are chewed over as they unfold, snap judgments race by in a blur, conventional wisdom hardens like so much ready-mix cement. Quick: Did Bill Clinton do the right thing or fall on his face? Will the Republicans gain the upper hand next week? On a scale of zero to ten, what are the chances that Congress will solve the health care crisis? Balance the budget? Find a cure for cancer? Complicated national and international issues are tossed into this journalistic Cuisinart and churned into high-speed pronouncements.

When Clinton ordered a bombing strike against Iraq in 1993, White House officials were stunned to see the pundits on *The Capital Gang* debating the political fallout even before the administration knew whether the bombs had landed. The talk had preempted the action itself. It is a dizzying process that provokes and titillates and entertains but, with some exceptions, rarely illuminates. And this mentality is increasingly spreading to print journalism, as exemplified by *Newsweek*'s "Conventional Wisdom Watch" and *Time*'s "Winners and Losers" column.

This is bad news for journalism, but more important, it's frequently bad for the country. The talk culture affects the business of governance in insidious ways. After the Sunday talk shows, senior White House advisers—George Stephanopoulos, James Carville, Paul Begala—get on the phone and assess whether the administration did well or got creamed that morning. Politicians of every persuasion grow obsessed with "winning the week," as reflected by the scorecard mentality of the weekend shows. Short-term maneuvering becomes more important than long-term policy. The political effort to "sell" an initiative on the talk circuit begins to overshadow the substance of the proposal itself. The talk show environment has given us a talk show government, presided over at the moment by the talkiest president of modern times. Journalists and politicians jabber at each other while the country slowly sinks into a morass of social and economic problems. The spectacle has fueled the cynicism of an electorate that sees the yawning chasm between this unceasing talk and the lack of tangible progress in their daily lives.

Talk Show Politicians

The triumph of talk has also produced the rise of the talk show candidate. Only in late-twentieth-century America would Patrick Buchanan, whose primary experience is popping off on radio and television, be treated as a serious presidential candidate, a status conferred in part by his appearances on the very shows for which he previously played the role of journalist. Buchanan was joined in the 1996 presidential race by Alan Keyes, a Baltimore radio talk show host and former Reagan administration official who stayed on the air for months even while campaigning, and by Representative Robert Dornan, a former California radio personality and regular Rush Limbaugh substitute. Ross Perot sought the presidency in 1992 almost exclusively by making the talk show rounds and spending part of his fortune on television ads. Talking, campaigning, and governing have become almost indistinguishable in this chattering age.

The hypercritical talk climate is not entirely new, of

course; much of the press has been abusive and ill-mannered toward political leaders for more than two centuries. . . . The Connecticut *Courant* said [Thomas Jefferson's] election would mean that "murder, robbery, rape, adultery and incest will openly be taught and practised." Abraham Lincoln was called an "ape," a "gorilla," and a "monster." Andrew Johnson was described as an "insolent, clownish creature" by the *New York World*. Grover Cleveland had to own up to reports that he had fathered an illegitimate child. Franklin Roosevelt was assailed on the radio by Father Charles Coughlin as a "liar," "betrayer," "scab," and "anti-God." John Kennedy was so incensed by the *New York Herald Tribune* that he canceled his subscription.

But news traveled more slowly in the pre-CNN era. Lincoln and FDR didn't have to worry about winning the week. Imagine what *The McLaughlin Group* would have said after Union troops were routed at Manassas, or how *The Capital Gang* would have jumped on the bombing of Pearl Harbor. Kennedy defused the Cuban missile crisis in 1962 by ignoring a harsh diplomatic note from Nikita Khrushchev and answering a second, more conciliatory letter. Today someone would leak word of the first note, one hundred White House reporters would demand a response, and Ted Koppel would race on the air with a "Cuba Held Hostage" special. "The constant drumbeat of news has an incalculable effect on the process of decision making," Stephanopoulos says. The political imperative is to do something—anything—to seize the initiative and quiet the catcalls, at least until the following week. . . .

News Becomes Tabloid TV

"What's good TV and what's thoughtful analysis are different," [says talk-show regular Margaret Carlson]. "That's been conceded by most producers and bookers. They're not looking for the most learned person; they're looking for the person who can sound learned without confusing the matter with too much knowledge. I'm one of the people without too much knowledge. I'm perfect!"

The explosion of talk shows is part of an information revolution that now processes more news and commentary than ever before. People read newsletters hot off the fax machine, watch congressional hearings on C-SPAN, scan databases on wafer-thin CD-ROMs, sound off on America Online bulletin boards, download files from the Internet. Yet in early 1995, only half of Americans could identify the relentlessly publicized Newt Gingrich as speaker of the House, while 64 percent knew that Lance Ito was the judge in the O.J. Simpson trial. We are drowning in information, increasingly unable to make sense of the waves of onrushing data. The talk shows are merely the loudest element, overloading our circuits with chatter that ranges from profound to profoundly trivial.

The talk culture has been further vulgarized by the popularity of tabloid television, which increasingly has set the agenda for the mainstream media. Marla Maples [the mistress of millionaire Donald Trump] discusses her love life with Diane Sawyer on *PrimeTime Live*. Paula Jones [who sued President Clinton for sexual harassment] dishes to Sam Donaldson. Gennifer Flowers [who made headlines during the 1992 presidential election as Clinton's alleged mistress] is carried live on CNN. [Disgraced former figure skater] Tonya Harding appears on *Inside Edition* and *Eye to Eye with Connie Chung*. John Bobbitt does *American Journal* and *Now with Tom Brokaw and Katie Couric*. Lorena Bobbitt tells her penis-chopping tale to *20/20*. All the shows compete for the endless parade of O.J. relatives, friends, lawyers, and hangers-on, and finally for Simpson himself, despite all the evidence that he committed two brutal murders.

In this tawdry environment, criminals become just another kind of celebrity to be booked, interviewed, and promoted. Diane Sawyer chats up Charles Manson on *PrimeTime Live*, just as Geraldo Rivera and others have over the years. *Dateline NBC* debriefs Jeffrey Dahmer. Paul Hill, who killed a doctor and his bodyguard at a Florida abortion clinic, turns up with Phil Donahue and Vladimir Posner. Colin Ferguson, who shot up a Long Island commuter train, gets his moment in the spotlight on *Today* and *Larry King Live*. On the talk circuit, even mass murderers are stars. The more gruesome the crime, the better the ratings.

Hosts Wield Power

The high priests of talk—Larry King, John McLaughlin, Rush Limbaugh, Don Imus, Phil Donahue, Oprah Winfrey, Ted Koppel—wield unprecedented power, reaching millions with their daily gabfests. While commentators in the age of Walter Lippmann or James Reston sought mainly to influence the governing elite, the new talkmeisters play to the masses. Presidents and prime ministers and putative leaders rush to appear on their programs because the hosts are presumed to be in touch with the public, as measured by Nielsen and Arbitron numbers that certify who is hot and who's not.

Yet the range of "debate" that unfolds on most television programs is almost laughably narrow. Few panelists challenge the underlying assumptions of official Washington; any argument that lacks significant support in Congress is blown off the radar screen as irrelevant. Problems that fall out of fashion with the Beltway establishment (say, homelessness) cease to exist on television, while issues that are in favor (say, family values) consume plenty of airtime. Problems ignored by Congress (say, the savings and loan crisis) hit the talk circuit only after they explode into scandal.

Many of those who yak for a living exist in a hermetically sealed cocoon, rubbing shoulders only with other affluent insiders and leaving town only to speak to paying audiences. They pontificate about welfare but have never actually spoken to a welfare mother. They hold forth on the decline of manufacturing but have never set foot in a factory, except perhaps with a politician on a handshaking tour. Firsthand knowledge or shoe-leather reporting is not a prerequisite in the talk world. With a few notable exceptions, such as *Charlie Rose* or *Nightline,* just popping off fills the bill quite nicely.

The pundit lineup tilts noticeably to the right: Michael Kinsley is charged with upholding the liberal cause on *Crossfire,* though he is not nearly as far to the left as Pat Buchanan is to the right. But Christian conservatives and far-right spokesmen are also largely excluded. Few blacks and Hispanics fill the regular pundit chairs, and the relative handful of women underscores their token status. The punditocracy is a testosterone-driven calling.

To be sure, many of those who blab for a living are smart and savvy folks, yet they must tailor their performances to the imperatives of the camera and the microphone. I understand the seductions of this culture all too well, . . . for although I make my primary living behind a word processor, I have gradually become part of the endless parade of talking heads. I have basked in the ego-warming glow of the klieg lights, struggling to sound sage while wrestling with the limitations of the format.

Cyberpunks and Junk Food

J.C. Herz

As personal computers became as ubiquitous as television sets in a majority of American homes, journalist J.C. Herz contends that a new generation of Internet-savvy children have developed their own subcultures on-line. These cyber surfers, says Herz, dissect everything from the latest movie plots to what sort of food to eat for breakfast.

I've been spending a lot of time on alt.cyberpunk. There's nothing like watching a once-underground subculture twitch through the wrenching throes of self-definition in the glare of media attention. (Cyberpunk: the *Time* cover story. Cyberpunk, the Billy Idol album. Can lunch boxes and action figures be far behind?) Cyberpunk science fiction, as written by authors like William Gibson and Bruce Sterling, is beloved of the Net community because it makes heroes out of techie outcasts. The skinny, disheveled, worn-down outsider takes on the Bad Guys. He's got a computer. They've got hired mercenaries. And the tech-savvy street rat wins every time. Cyberpunk glamorizes the hacker. It's every computer nerd's fantasy. But whether it's a bona fide "movement" is a subject of some contention, particularly on alt.cyberpunk. And right now, members of this movement, if it does indeed exist, are crash-testing various manifestos. *Line Noiz*, an electronic 'zine on alt.cyberpunk, runs a know-it-when-you-see-it definition culled from the newsgroup's list of frequently asked questions (FAQ):

So, what makes a cyberpunk? [If] you're laughing at my generalities and inconsistencies, then you're definitely a cyberpunk. If you're a techno-junkie or an info-junkie, then you'd probably consider yourself a cyberpunk. Basically, if you live in a world in the not-so-distant-future, ahead of the masses (the masses being guys named Buford who sit out in front of their trailer homes in lawn chairs sipping a Bud and watching the Indy 500 on an old TV), then you could probably safely consider yourself a cyberpunk. . . .

This is a clever bid for credibility on the part of *Line Noiz*, seeing as how it grandfathers its entire readership into the movement and shies from the riptide of specificity. It's not the broad brushstrokes that induce apoplexy around here. It's the efforts of self-appointed cyberstyle mavens to retrofit a fashion statement from the pages of [cyber magazine] *Mondo 2000*. Trying to label albums, hairstyles, and footwear with the Cyberpunk seal of approval only triggers more confusion and paranoia. Basically, all hell has broken loose now that this motley pack has to deal with fitting in here, of all places. Cyberpunk, after all, has everything to do with the glorification of misfits.

Cyber Junk Food

When hackers—never renowned for their fashion sense—start posting sartorial advice, it's time to worry.

After the newsmagazine blitzkrieg, the ideological free fall continues for months. Finally, it hits bottom; an Australian university student takes the categorization fiesta to its logical extreme: "Just wondering," he asks, "what would people consider to be Cyberpunk food??"

Such a short, innocent question, such a seemingly simple issue—like the border of Alsace-Lorraine or the eternal tastes-great-less-filling controversy—touches off a firestorm whose bitterness is only heightened by its absurdity.

Snack food. Somehow, the churning self-examination of an entire subculture has come down to "cheap fast food, potato chips, junk food, liberally sparsed with psychedelics," the nomination from a netter in Washington State, seconded by a scattered multitude of North Americans. I sit back and wonder why a pack of brainiac individualists has suddenly decided to use snack food preference as a proxy for collective identity. What the hell are these people trying to do by defining themselves in terms of [convenience store] dry goods? As I follow the snack food issue over the Net, the phrase "You are what you eat" takes on frightening connotations.

"Woke up today 5 minutes after i was supposed to be to work," writes Teknikl, a hacker with a Sisyphean computer graphics job—indexing binary pictures of cracks in highway pavement. Woke up today—don't all blues songs start that way? I half expect Tek to continue in twelve-bar verse form like Charlie Patton in cyberspace.

"Damn, i thought to myself, now i don't get any breakfast. This isn't really a big problem, since the quickmart is across the street, waiting patiently to sell me more coffee creamer and those nasty little cakes they sell at quickmarts that aren't part of larger chains. Little debbies, ultranasty 'kooshpies' made by twisted locals who think they've invented a new food type, and those ugly pecan pies. I really didn't want any of this stuff . . . I needed food."

Ho-Hos® and Caffeine

Clearly, cheapness and low nutritional value are essential to the cyberpunk snack food gestalt. Mark Gooley, the cult hero of alt.non.sequitur, advises his flock to embrace artificial ingredients in one of his inimitable Gooley nonsense sermons:

"Aspartame by the plateful! Hateful plateful, careful carful, icky knickers? The movement started in Puerto Rico about ten minutes ago and is spreading inch-thick layers of Simplesse (tm), as written by Grimmelshausen, on every major highway in the United States except for those with prime-number names. Ever had roast Beat Poet? . . . Beer doesn't love me any more."

As the snack food thread spins out on various newsgroups, malnutrition acquires a grungy chic, and the nethead diaspora begins to riff on a white trash convenience store motif: Ding Dongs, Ho-Hos, and Grandma's cookies. Cyberpunk snack food is invariably described as single-serving, individually wrapped for the alienated and hard-up. Salty, carcinogenic tide-over food, redolent of dehydro-genated soybean oil, downward mobility, and creeping retail homogenization, would surely represent the post-apocalyptic future. . . . Chemical side effects on the brain are an added bonus. Stimulants in general, and caffeinated beverages in particular, are cataloged in detail that veers between science and poetry.

Indeed, the Net is probably the only place where a comparison of the caffeine content in instant, drip, and ex-presso coffee, Twining's English Breakfast tea, Jolt cola, Swiss Miss hot chocolate, and Mountain Dew, in moles per liter, is not considered comprehensive. Multicultural netters wired on Chinese bark extracts have to chip in their two cents. Prescription diehards lobby for vasopressin. ("No letdown, just instant wakey-wakey. Does dry out yer nasal cavities though. Bummer.") This kind of discussion contin-ues till dawn. He who stays awake longest wins. Long after I've thrown in the towel, an electronic cry of triumph rings across the Net: "Pills. Teas. Carbonated beverages. Ama-teur SLOTH!!!!!!" Apparently, some guy has engineered an intravenous ephedrine drip.

Anthems of Alternative Music

Pat Blashill

The word *alternative* was used by the media in the 1990s to describe teenage culture much the way *rock and roll* was used in previous decades. In this selection Pat Blashill, a contributing editor of *Details* magazine and the author of many articles about the music scene and popular culture, points out that the rather bland word *alternative* has been used to describe everything from pierced, tattooed, and skateboarding cyberpunks to extremely popular bands such as Pearl Jam. But, in Blashill's opinion, the punky attitudes found in alternative culture were the voices of disaffected teenagers attempting to distance themselves from the insipid consumer pop culture of the late twentieth century.

Use the word "alternative" around anyone under twenty-five, and you will see that kid wince. It's the instinctual shudder of someone rejecting a pat definition of his generation. "Alternative" may be the only word we have to describe a culture that straggled up through the cracks in the pavement of Main Street, but somehow it's not enough. Never before has a word as colorless as "alternative" been bandied about to describe such a crazy panoply of best-selling musical artists, including everyone from an odd, confessional singer/songwriter named Liz Phair to a martini-swilling glam-rock band called Urge Overkill. Never before has a word been so inadequate and *over-*

---

stretched and carelessly applied to such a broad spectrum of cultural phenomena as suburban skateboarding, mall tattoo parlors, the rise of fanzines, and the popularity of home-grown, independent films like *Clerks*. And never before has such an unappetizing word been employed to sell youth culture back to the people who invented it in the first place. Besides, "alternative" is now a misnomer.

Anthem of Disaffection

Today alternative describes the tastes and predilections of mainstream American youth. But alternative culture wasn't invented by Nirvana in 1992. They just brought an anthem of disaffection and anger to the top of the charts, to the malls, to the army bases, and into the living rooms of a nation that had spent most of the eighties trying to convince itself that it was a kind and gentle place.

In the eighties, America was all about shiny surfaces, and mainstream culture was about as deep as Bobby Mc-Ferrin's 1988 hit song, "Don't Worry, Be Happy." Movies like *Back to the Future* and *Romancing the Stone* weren't the norm, just sure signs that Hollywood was again becoming a factory for empty escapism. The best-seller lists were rocked by *Slaves of New York, Less Than Zero, Bright Lights, Big City*, three very hip novels about people with nice clothes, cocaine, and hardly anything to say.

Alternative culture in this country began as an attempt to get to the truth and beauty beneath the polished surfaces of American mainstream thought and art. This wasn't a new impulse—it was the very same mission that has driven bohemian underground movements, both here and abroad, throughout this century.

Warm, Human Sound

So what does it mean today to see Pearl Jam's Eddie Vedder wearing a Minor Threat punk-rock T-shirt? It means that he is acting out one of the most inexorable impulses of indie rock—that is, the fiendish desire to turn anyone who will listen on to something new: a band they might not have heard, a magazine they didn't know about, a snowboard shop they've never seen. It means that Eddie is a fan, not just someone who inspires fans. The rock T-shirt is the sartorial shorthand of our generation. It says, "I like this music—I am this culture." No other explanation from the wearer is necessary.

Alternative music makes virtues out of the vices that mainstream pop and rock previously tried to avoid. The bands use guitar distortion not just as a musical device, but as a medium unto itself, and they make noise that is as expressive as a playground melody. They use murky production and effects as a way of evoking atmosphere. They play with old drum kits and transistor amplifiers because that gives the music a warm, human sound. Because of these

Nirvana Puts Alternative Music on the Charts

The rise of Nirvana and the suicide of the band's leader, Kurt Cobain, was the music story of the decade. Cobain's antiestablishment attitude and complete rejection of American society ironically made him an overnight success worth tens of millions of dollars. Cobain attempted to kill his mental anguish with heroin, and when that no longer worked, he killed himself with a shotgun.

"All I need is a break, and my stress will be over with," says Cobain. "I'm going to get healthy and start over." He's certainly earned a break after playing nearly 100 dates on four continents in five months, never staying in one place long enough for a doctor to tend to his stomach problem. And he and his band mates, bassist Krist Novoselic and drummer Dave Grohl, have had to cope with the peculiar position of being the world's first triple-platinum punk-rock band.

Soon after the September release of *Nevermind*, MTV pumped "Teen Spirit" night and day as the album vaulted up the charts things, alternative rock *sounds* like the polar opposite of the ultraslick top pop that dominated radio and MTV in the eighties. This music, much of which was released initially on independent labels and played to small but fervent audiences, is no longer an underground phenomenon. Yet texturally, it still sounds slightly subterranean, like something repressed that crawled up from beneath the boards of the American bandstand. In a sense, this is still underground music because it sounds, feels, and looks dirty.

The Underside of Bland

The same idea applies to everything in alternative or indie culture besides the music. Indie style—the clothes, the poster art for concerts, the movies that Nirvana fans embrace—is

---

until it hit No. 1. Although the band's label, DGC, doubted the album would sell over 250,000 copies, it sold 3 million in just four months and continues to sell nearly 100,000 copies a week.

For Nirvana, putting out their first major-label record was like getting into a new car. But the runaway success was like suddenly discovering that the car was a Ferrari and the accelerator pedal was Krazy Glued to the floorboard. Friends worried about how the band was dealing with it all.

"Dave's just psyched," says Nils Bernstein, a good friend of the band members' who coordinates their fan mail. "He's 22, and he's a womanizer, and he's just: '*Score!*'" Novoselic, according to Bernstein, had a drinking problem but went on the wagon this year.

But rumors are flying about Cobain. A recent item in the music-industry magazine *Hits* said Cobain was "slam dancing with Mr. Brownstone," Guns 'N Roses slang for doing heroin. A January profile in *BAM* magazine claimed that Cobain was "nodding off in mid-sentence," adding "the pinned pupils, sunken cheeks and scabbed, sallow skin suggest something more serious than mere fatigue."

Editors of *Rolling Stone, Cobain.* Boston: Little, Brown, 1994.

all about entropy, about the underside of a bland Norman Rockwell dream. That's why Hüsker Dü titled one of their albums *Everything Falls Apart*. That's why White Zombie fans dress like the band—with matted dreadlocks, dirty-ass torn jeans, and motorcycle boots taped together with duct tape. That's why a major studio movie like *Reality Bites*, produced to appeal to and exploit alternative-rock fans, features a key scene in a convenience store, the quintessential marketplace of nineties fast-food garbage culture. And that's why long hair, originally a sign of effeminate defiance, is now almost purely a gesture of evasion, refusal and disengagement. Worn by an indie rock kid, long hair is just a shade, a mess that obscures the boy's eyes, his motives, maybe even his dreams. As if to say that these things couldn't possibly matter to anyone else.

This culture was and is still about going out to a club to see a band and your friends. It's a social scene. It's community. It's about reading Peter Bagge's comic *Hate*, or yucking it up online with other fans, and it's about understanding what everyone's talking about because you've seen that new band too. Or because you've lent your couch to the same kind of loser in a Veruca Salt T-shirt who seems to move from town to town, scamming his way into shows for free and mooching beer money from everyone.

This is a community that began as a series of local music scenes, as the sort of little subcultural eddies that guys with pierced noses and goatees call "temporary autonomous zones." A T.A.Z. is really just any place you can go to hear your own kind of music, while wearing the fashions of your chosen tribe and drinking the cocktail beverages of your generation. It's any scene in which you can be certain that you are not just like your parents. Over the last decade, these little sites of youth culture began to link up, city by city, like a foundation of slightly scuffed-up Lego blocks, by sharing local heroes, ideas, and records with each other.

Women Rockers Thrive at the Lilith Fair

Robert Hilburn

The success of alternative rock generated alternative rock festivals. The first such festival was the multicultural Lollapalooza, which combined rap, punk, metal, and a wide variety of other musical styles. Lollapalooza was first established in the summer of 1991 by Jane's Addiction singer Perry Farrell.

In 1997 Sarah McLachlan proved that women rock shows could draw huge crowds. The singer defied conventional wisdom and began producing the all-female Lilith Fair, featuring a who's who of award-winning women rockers. Despite industry warnings that an all-female roster would not sell tickets, *Los Angeles Times* music critic Robert Hilburn points out that Lilith grossed $16 million in thirty-eight shows, nearly doubling the take of the male-dominated Lollapalooza. A two-disc album, featuring live performances from Lilith, grossed another $4 million.

Sarah McLachlan has heard most of the condescending names that male music biz insiders coined after she announced [1997's] all-female Lilith Fair festival tour.

The 30-year-old singer-songwriter even smiles now at the mention of them: "Girlapalooza"..."Lesbopalooza"... and the rest.

Excerpted from "They Said She Couldn't Do It," by Robert Hilburn, *Los Angeles Times,* June 21, 1998. Reprinted with permission from the *Los Angeles Times.*

When it gets to one she hasn't heard, she breaks into a flat-out laugh: "Breastfest."

"Oh, my God," she says, cackling during an interview here. "Really. Well, there you go."

Then again, it's easy for McLachlan to laugh these days.

Despite industry warnings that an all-female roster wouldn't be viable, the Lilith tour grossed more than $16 million in 38 shows. That's nearly $500,000 a stop—easily outstripping the $294,000 average [1997 gross] of Lolla-palooza, the summer's high-testosterone, alt-rock affair, according to trade publication *Pollstar*.

Based on that success, Lilith is expanding to 57 U.S. shows [in 1998]. . . . After the U.S. dates, Lilith plans to test the market in Europe, Australia and Japan. Potential gross on the U.S. dates alone this time around: more than $25 million.

A two-disc Lilith album—featuring live performances from such 1997 tour participants as McLachlan, Paula Cole and Jewel—has grossed another $4 million since its release April 28, 1998.

This all adds up to a major breakthrough for female artists, who for decades have been viewed as secondary players in the male-dominated pop world. For years, radio and record executives believed there was such limited demand for female artists that companies had informal quotas. Where labels would typically sign dozens of male rock bands, they might sign just one female rock band each. Radio stations also generally limited the number of female artists on their playlists—and almost never programmed two records by women back to back.

Freshest Music of the 1990s

Women, however, have become an increasingly powerful part of the record market over the last decade, as demonstrated by such mainstream artists such as Whitney Houston and Celine Dion as well as more cutting-edge ones, including rock's Alanis Morissette and hip-hop's Erykah Badu. Radio airplay has reflected this.

One reason for this commercial clout is that women over the last decade have become the biggest purchasers of music—up from 43% in 1988 to 51.4% [in 1997], reports the Recording Industry Assn. of America. At the same time, female artists arguably have made the freshest music in the '90s.

Lilith—which drew 70% women, mostly ages 18 to 35—finally brought the concert business to the celebration.

"We always knew that it wasn't true . . . that it was just sexist to think you couldn't have women on the same bill," says three-time Grammy winner Shawn Colvin in a separate interview. "It was just a matter of time before it would be proven false, and I'm only glad I was around when it happened. It's like an albatross being taken off your neck."

McLachlan, who won a best female pop vocal Grammy in 1998 for her recording of "Building a Mystery," agrees.

"Sure, I was pissed at one point over all the [names for Lilith], but then I realized that it's all just silly," she says.

"When we first started doing this, they said it wouldn't work because women don't buy tickets and don't buy T-shirts and on and on. And there was all this talk about what a risk we were taking. Well, I guess I am just naive because I didn't see it as that. I knew women liked music . . . and guess what? I was right.". . .

McLachlan tends to downplay her importance in the Lilith story, but she is the guiding spirit behind the affair, everyone involved acknowledges. She either came up with or signed off on all the key decisions, from the women-only nature of the show to the sizable charity component.

Each of the 57 concerts will feature five (or more) performers on the main stage, with half a dozen or so others on the smaller support stages. Only McLachlan will appear on each show.

Among the headliners who'll be along for part of the tour: Erykah Badu, Natalie Merchant, Missy "Misdemeanor" Elliott, Paula Cole, Bonnie Raitt, Emmylou Harris, the Fugees' Lauryn Hill, Meshell Ndegéocello and Liz Phair. It's a much more diverse lineup than in 1997. The support stages will also offer such critical or commercial favorites as country music's Martina McBride, dance-accented folk stylist Beth Orton and hip-hop newcomer Imani Coppola. Altogether, more than 50 artists will perform in a remarkable showcase of contemporary talent. . . .

A Celebration of Women and Music

In many ways, McLachlan—whose radiant smile and easy, engaging laugh contrast sharply with the shy, waif-like image of her early album cover photos—is an unlikely heroine for the Lilith story.

If you had drafted a list of 20 women most likely to take the leadership role in putting together pop's first female music festival, it's doubtful that you would have thought of the Canadian.

The Halifax native doesn't have the missionary zeal of [Sinead] O'Connor (who is "thrilled" to be joining the tour in 1998) or the historical standing of Patti Smith (who performed in 1997) or the camp-fire enthusiasm of the Indigo Girls (both 1997 and 1998) or the headline-grabbing bravado of Courtney Love (who praises Lilith as an important step for women and says she'd love to join the event some year).

Ironically, it is the absence of those qualities that made McLachlan such a good candidate to sponsor Lilith. If she had too high a media profile or too strong a political agenda or too much acclaim or too much of a sales record, she might have been viewed as a competitor and scared others away.

Instead, she's someone whom other artists respect and feel safe with.

Emily Saliers, half of the Indigo Girls, only knew McLachlan by her music before the duo joined the tour last year, but she was impressed by McLachlan's spirit and commitment.

"At first in the press conferences, I think Sarah was kind of finding her way around the issues, . . . things like the purpose of the tour, whether there should be men on it [as lead performers]," Saliers says. "Over time, she became very solid in her beliefs and about the tour. She saw it as a celebration of women and music, especially music."

Melissa Miller, vice president of booking for Universal Concerts Talent, which operates the Universal Amphi-theatre and 11 other venues in North America, also lauds McLachlan.

"Sarah's not the shy, quiet individual that many people think," she says. "She is a very strong, very self-assured, very intelligent woman who doesn't need to go out to the world and prove she is someone. She just is. I wasn't surprised that she would be the one to make [Lilith] happen.". . .

Playful, Spirited McLachlan

It's this playful, spirited side of McLachlan that has often been lost over the years—partly because she keeps a low media profile.

Spend even a few minutes with her and you'll be treated to her candor and her sometimes earthy language.

She'll tell you about the dream in which she was turned into Courtney Love at a church revival meeting. . . . And she'll explain why some of the songs on 1997's album, "Surfacing," had such a dark, troubled edge.

The short version is that she broke up with one band member (he's no longer in the group) and fell in love with another (he's now her husband). The long version adds that the new boyfriend was her best girlfriend's ex boy-friend, a situation that greatly strained the women's rela-tionship for months.

Even with all this potential tabloid fodder, however, McLachlan continues to be thought of by much of the pop world as a somewhat delicate waif.

"It's like people have this certain image of me and they don't want to change it," she says. "It's so funny actually. In the early days, I was so shy, I didn't even look at the camera or smile. I think a lot of it had to do with not feel-ing very sure of myself.

"So, when I went to Japan not too long ago, I started

smiling and looking at the camera and the photographers all went, 'Oh, no, no . . . please don't do that.' They wanted that shy, demure, subservient image."

Not that she seems to care that much.

"For one thing, I live in Canada," she offers in explanation of the media profile. "I suppose if I were living in some place like L.A. and going out to all the openings and being seen around town, I'd probably be written about a lot more.

"But I love Canada. I've never felt drawn to move to L.A. or New York. My friends and family are here, and I'm needy in that way. I love having people I'm close to near me."

McLachlan was born in Halifax in 1968, one of three otherwise non-related children adopted at an early age by a pair of Americans who moved to Nova Scotia, where the husband was a marine biologist.

Though she felt loved by her parents, she had a difficult time fitting in at school. She was often called ugly by her classmates and she withdrew. Music and art were her two comforts.

As a child, she listened a lot to her mother's Joan Baez and Simon & Garfunkel albums and her dad's jazz albums. By her mid-teens, however, she became obsessive about her own discoveries, including Peter Gabriel and Kate Bush, as well as the occasional album by such other favorites as Willie Nelson, Rickie Lee Jones and Tom Waits.

She figured art was an easier path because she had no idea how to get started in the music business. She did a little bit of singing around town with a new wave band during art school, and that led to a contract from Nettwerk.

Terry McBride, a partner in the label and its related management company, says he was intrigued by the teenager's personality. "I've always said there are a lot of great singers, but not a lot of great personalities," he says now. "There was this spark there the way she talked about things."

The first album, 1988's "Touch," didn't make much of a

stir in the U.S., but the second, 1992's "Solace," was embraced both by critics and radio programmers. One reason was that the best moments reflected an intense exposition reminiscent of O'Connor, whose "I Do Not Want What I Haven't Got" album that year opened a wide door for strong, introspective female voices.

The next album, 1994's "Fumbling Towards Ecstasy," was her commercial breakthrough, thanks to exhaustive touring and widespread airplay for "Possession," a single about an obsessed fan.

McLachlan was suddenly in a strong enough position as a live draw to name her own opening act. For the last leg of the "Fumbling" tour, she decided on a relative newcomer named Paula Cole. Little did McLachlan know that this decision would lead to the formation of Lilith Fair.

Opening the Door for Women

It has been customary for years in the music world for proven headliners to choose their opening acts. Sometimes they pick an act as a favor to a record company or manager who is looking for exposure for a new artist. Sometimes they do it with an idea of adding variety or to add drawing power to the bill.

In McLachlan's case, she chose Cole in the spring of 1996 because she liked the singer-songwriter's music.

So, she wasn't happy when word started filtering back that some promoters thought it wasn't a good idea to have two women on the show. Couldn't she rethink it, some suggested. "It wasn't across the board, but there was a definite reaction . . . some definite heat," recalls booking agent Marty Diamond.

McLachlan's answer was firm.

She wanted Cole and her own team of advisors—including manager McBride and tour manager Dan Fraser—to come up with a plan where they would, in effect, call the promoters' bluff.

Instead of the normal concert guarantee, McLachlan would assume all the risk. She would take 80% of the gross and give the promoter 20% as a handling fee.

The dates, mostly in 2,000- and 3,000-seat halls, not only sold out, but the spirit at the shows was so strong that McLachlan came up with the idea of adding some more female artists to four shows in the summer of 1996. One of them, at the 5,000-seat Starlight Bowl in Burbank, featured McLachlan, Cole and Suzanne Vega, and sold out in advance.

By the time of the final series of shows in Vancouver, McLachlan and her team had come up with the name Lilith and had begun experimenting with eventual Lilith features, including a second stage and a "village" of vendors and information booths.

When Lilith was being scheduled in early 1997, Universal's Melissa Miller believed in the concept so much that she talked Universal into helping to underwrite the tour by signing up for several shows across the country.

"I didn't think it was a risk, but [the Lilith organizers] did face [some] promoters who were fearful of the concept," she says now. "The success of the tour didn't just open a door for women, but I hope it encouraged everyone in our business to be a bit more open-minded . . . to be more willing to take chances. As an industry, we need that."

If the Lilith box-office figures were strong from the start, the spirit of the show took a while to evolve. Critics complained in the early dates that there wasn't enough interaction between the performers—just a series of individual sets.

That changed when the Indigo Girls came aboard about three weeks into the two-month journey.

"They were an amazing influence," McLachlan recalls. "We are all a little bit shy, a little bit hesitant to go up to someone you don't know and go, 'Hey, I love your music, can I play with you?' It's like asking someone on a date. You don't want to get turned down. But Amy [Ray] and Emily did it and they made you want to join in. They lifted the tour to another level."

Besides making promoters and fans happy, the tour donated $1 from every ticket to local charities and is responsible, through sponsorship deals, for supporting all sorts of other social causes.

"I'm 39 so I wasn't really around in the '60s, but I like to think that it was something like this, . . . this spirit," says agent Diamond. "I like to think this tour is making a difference in a world of corporate mergers and buyouts and sellouts and one-hit wonders and all the cynicism."

CHAPTER 6

Science and Technology into the Twenty-First Century

Instant Communications Across Cyberspace

Joe Saltzman

By 1998 more than 45 million people were wired into the World Wide Web, allowing people to shop, tour art museums, and listen to their favorite band—all without leaving home. Although some in the 1980s predicted the end of the written word, *USA Today* editor Joe Saltzman contends that the Internet has actually permitted people of similar interests to instantly communicate with each other by reading and writing. Never before have so many people typed so many words to each other with such ease. Joe Saltzman is associate mass media editor of *USA Today* and associate director of the journalism school at the University of Southern California.

They didn't give the written word a chance to survive in the late 20th century. The new multimedia, digital world of the future was supposed to include plenty of dazzling images and sounds whose visual and aural environment didn't need the out-of-fashion written word. Words on paper were obsolete. Throw out all your books. The new computer-video world didn't need them anymore. How wrong could the soothsayers be? The written word is not only alive and well, but dominating the new media with a vengeance. Never in history have so many people written so much. Billions of words are written down each day by people with access to the Internet. Millions of pages of paper are printed each day by those who want a permanent keepsake of what flashes across their computer screens.

People sit for hours reading words on their computer screens. They read e-mail messages. They read newspaper and magazine articles. They read how-to manuals, medical journals, catalogues, and advertisements. They read about their favorite movies, actors, and musicians. They find whatever they are looking for in electronic stores and auctions. They read about new worlds and old passions. They read what search engines throw out at them on every con-

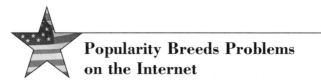

Popularity Breeds Problems on the Internet

In this excerpt, Brett Arquette, a freelance columnist and the chief technology officer for the Ninth Judicial Circuit Court in Orlando, Florida, contends that the exploding popularity of the Internet has created problems as well as blessings for the average user. Arquette believes that the Net is becoming so polluted with advertising, pornography, and game playing that its usefulness as an educational tool is being destroyed.

As the Internet grows in popularity, users are being swamped by useless links. . . . Year by year, I've noticed that the Internet is becoming profoundly polluted, and if the industry doesn't figure out a way to clean it up, it will become a glorified game-playing, spam-advertising, sex-pandering, fraud-inducing chat room. Or are we already too late?

The Internet is continually collecting more waste products— specifically dead links and moved Web sites. Each time I run a search on one of the major search engines, at least a quarter of the returned links are dead. If the search engine administrators can't find a way to clean out the dead links the search process will become so frustrating that people with deadlines simply

ceivable subject. The written word may be supplemented with fantastic images and audio segments, but it is the written word that is dominant. It is the written word that runs the current communication revolution.

Writing Again Without Pen and Paper

When doomsayers predicted the end of the written word, they apparently were thinking too much about television and not enough about the Internet. They saw that experiments asking consumers to "read" text on the TV screen were dismal failures. No one, it seemed, wanted to sit and read written words on a TV monitor. Then computers became the modern way to communicate. People began get-

---

won't have time to use it.

As millions of pages per day are pumped out on to the Internet, the art of finding what you want has become a lesson in futility. Why do search engines keep "advanced" search pages behind the initial search pages? Do they think that everyone initially wants to do a really bad search and pull up 3,000 pages of garbage? . . .

Now that most [Internet service providers] provide the ability for everyone to have his or her own home page, the flood of poorly updated and managed pages is creating a navigation nightmare. . . .

Can the Internet be saved from its own pollution? Probably not. Like flies in a glass bubble, its own contamination will eventually lead to its demise. In the next 10 years, the Internet will assume a role not unlike network television. Serious companies and businesses will splinter off to virtual private networks, similar to cable TV, where each person will be charged extra for access.

The Internet as we know it will go the way of the typewriter, becoming a once-valuable tool that's no longer efficient or productive—a catch-all conduit that only appeals to the lowest common denominator.

Brett Arquette, "Peer to Peer: Analysis of the Internet's Future," *InfoWorld*, December 7, 1998.

ting messages through e-mail and began favoring e-mail over phone calls. Unlike the phone call, an e-mail message does not interrupt life's flow. It can be answered at any time—even when the sender is asleep or unavailable.

E-mail correspondence became a convenient way to keep in touch with friends, acquaintances, people we hadn't seen for decades, people just met. The written message began to be the message of choice. You could write messages when you felt like writing them and you could make them as long or as short as you wanted. The recipient could read the message carefully or scroll through it rapidly without hurting your feelings. Without pen and paper, people started writing again. It is estimated that, in the 21st century, more people will correspond through e-mail than by the telephone. Some say the writing level on the Internet seems hopelessly juvenile, that the mauling of language and linguistics is appalling. We will end up a nation of very poor writers who excuse our illiteracy by arguing that electronic communication doesn't need the finesse and eloquence of written words on paper. It is true that anyone visiting a chat room on the Internet will find plenty of evidence to support that point of view.

But others might disagree. It is possible that the more people use the written word, the more skillful they will become at writing. The more they write, the more they will learn to appreciate the well-turned phrase, the arresting metaphor, the moving sentence. They will learn how to type and write faster and with more clarity. They will once again understand the power of the written word and its influence over people. They might even sit back, look at the screen, and marvel at the beauty of language.

Restoring Power to the User

Calling up information or messages on a computer screen puts the individual back in control. No fast-moving, impossible-to-understand TV news broadcast or electronic images that flash by in seconds. When you are in charge, you can linger over a delectable phrase or concept. You can re-read the information at your own pace. You can contemplate a response in the fullness of time. You can decide what to read and when to read it. It has restored power to the consumer.

The great surprise of these last few years of the 20th century is how much the great communications revolution has restored the ability of a single anonymous mind to pursue knowledge, rummage through the vast resources of civilization, and ferret out subjects usually reserved for scholars and collectors. Any written word typed into an Internet search engine can yield all kinds of other written words on obscure or popular subjects. You can search every conceivable publication available, roam through the great museums and libraries of the world, explore the databanks of governments and foundations, and bring all of the world's knowledge to your computer, courtesy of the written word.

So . . . the death of the written word has been greatly exaggerated. It seems that the written word is not only here to stay, but has become our gateway to knowledge and entertainment in ways Johannes Gutenberg, who invented printing from moveable type [in the fifteenth century], never imagined. No matter what joys or terror new technology has for us in the future, the old-fashioned written word will be there to witness, explain, explore, and help us understand who we were, who we are, and who we hope to be.

Personal Privacy Lost to Technology

David Brin

Technology brought many blessings and conveniences to the human race in the 1990s. But best-selling author and space physicist David Brin contends that there was a dark side to the technology: the growing widespread ability of the government—or anyone else—to use mini–video cameras, tiny microphones, and computers to gather personal information and spy on people. In this selection, Brin explores this loss of privacy and how it became a growing concern for those who understood the frightening capabilities of the new technology.

This is a tale of two cities. Cities of the near future, say ten or twenty years from now.

Barring something unforeseen, you are apt to be living in one of these two places. Your only choice may be which one.

At first sight, these two municipalities look pretty much alike. Both contain dazzling technological marvels, especially in the realm of electronic media. Both suffer familiar urban quandaries of frustration and decay. . . .

None of these features is of interest to us right now, for we have noticed something about both of these twenty-first-century cities that *is* radically different. A trait that marks them as distinct from any metropolis of the late 1990s.

Street crime has nearly vanished from both towns. But that is only a symptom, a result.

Video Cameras on Every Lamppost

The real change peers down from every lamppost, every rooftop and street sign.

Tiny cameras, panning left and right, survey traffic and pedestrians, observing everything in open view.

Have we entered an Orwellian nightmare? Have the burghers of both towns banished muggings at the cost of creating a [Communist] dystopia?

Consider city number one. In this place, all the myriad cameras report their urban scenes straight to Police Central, where security officers use sophisticated image processors to scan for infractions against public order—or perhaps against an established way of thought. Citizens walk the streets aware that any word or deed may be noted by agents of some mysterious bureau.

Now let's skip across space and time.

At first sight, things seem quite similar in city number two. Again, ubiquitous cameras perch on every vantage point. Only here we soon find a crucial difference. These devices do *not* report to the secret police. Rather, each and every citizen of this metropolis can use his or her wristwatch television to call up images from any camera in town.

Here a late-evening stroller checks to make sure no one lurks beyond the corner she is about to turn.

Over there a tardy young man dials to see if his dinner date still waits for him by a city fountain.

A block away, an anxious parent scans the area to find which way her child wandered off.

Over by the mall, a teenage shoplifter is taken into custody gingerly, with minute attention to ritual and rights, because the arresting officer knows that the entire process is being scrutinized by untold numbers who watch intently, lest her neutral professionalism lapse.

In city number two, such microcameras are banned from some indoor places . . . but not from police headquarters! There any citizen may tune in on bookings, arraignments, and especially the camera control room itself, making sure that the agents on duty look out for violent crime, and only crime.

Despite their initial similarity, these are very different cities, representing disparate ways of life, completely opposite relationships between citizens and their civic guardians. The reader may find both situations somewhat chilling. Both futures may seem undesirable. But can there be any doubt which city we'd rather live in, if these two make up our only choice?

The Future Has Arrived

Alas, they do appear to be our only options. For the cameras *are* on their way, along with data networks that will send myriad images flashing back and forth, faster than thought.

In fact, the future has already arrived. The trend began in Britain a decade ago, in the town of King's Lynn, where sixty remote-controlled video cameras were installed to scan known "trouble spots," reporting directly to police headquarters. The resulting reduction in street crime exceeded all predictions; in or near zones covered by surveillance, crime dropped to one-seventieth of the former rate. The savings in patrol costs alone paid for the equipment in a few months. Dozens of cities and towns soon followed the example of King's Lynn. Glasgow, Scotland, reported a 68 percent drop in crime citywide, while police in Newcastle fingered over 1,500 perpetrators with taped evidence. (All but seven pleaded guilty, and those seven were later convicted.) In May 1997, Newcastle soccer fans rampaged through downtown streets. Detectives studying video tapes picked out 152 faces and published 80 photographs in local newspapers. In days, all were identified.

Today, over 300,000 cameras are in place throughout the United Kingdom, transmitting round-the-clock images to a hundred constabularies, all of them reporting decreases in public misconduct. Polls report that the cameras are extremely popular with citizens, though British civil libertarian John Wadham and others have bemoaned this proliferation of snoop technology, claiming, "It could be used for any other purpose, and of course it could be abused."

Visitors to Japan, Thailand, and Singapore will see that other countries are rapidly following the British example, using closed circuit television (CCTV) to supervise innumerable public areas.

This trend was slower coming to North America, but it appears to be taking off. After initial experiments garnered widespread public approval, the City of Baltimore put police cameras to work scanning all 106 downtown intersections. In 1997, New York City began its own program to set up twenty-four-hour remote surveillance in Central Park, subway stations, and other public places.

No one denies the obvious and dramatic short-term benefits derived from this early proliferation of surveillance technology. That is not the real issue. In the long run, the sovereign folk of Baltimore and countless other communities will have to make the same choice as the inhabitants of our two mythical cities. *Who will ultimately control the cameras?*

Invisible Surveillance

Consider a few more examples.

How many parents have wanted to be a fly on the wall while their child was at day care? This is now possible with a new video monitoring system known as Kindercam, linked to high-speed telephone lines and a central Internet server. Parents can log on, type "www.kindercam.com," enter their password, and access a live view of their child in day care at any time, from anywhere in the world. Kindercam will be installed in two thousand day-care facilities nationwide by the end of 1998. Mothers on business trips, fathers who live out of state, even distant grandparents can all "drop in" on their child daily. Drawbacks? Overprotective parents may check compulsively. And now other parents can observe *your* child misbehaving!

Some of the same parents are less happy about the lensed

Reprinted with permission from Kirk Anderson.

pickups that are sprouting in their own workplaces, enabling supervisors to tune in on them in the same way they use Kindercam to check up on their kids.

That is, if they notice the cameras at all. At present, engineers can squeeze the electronics for a video unit into a package smaller than a sugar cube. Complete sets half the size of a pack of cigarettes were recently offered for sale by the Spy Shop, a little store in New York City located two blocks from the United Nations. Meanwhile, units with radio transmitters are being disguised in clock radios, telephones, and toasters, as part of the burgeoning "nannycam" trend. So high is demand for these pickups, largely by parents eager to check on their babysitters, that just one firm in Orange County, California, has recently been selling from five hundred to one thousand disguised cameras a month. By the end of 1997, prices had dropped from $2,500 to $399.

Cameras aren't the only surveillance devices proliferating in our cities. Starting with Redwood City, near San Francisco, several police departments have begun lacing neighborhoods with sound pickups that transmit directly back to headquarters. Using triangulation techniques, officials can now pinpoint bursts of gunfire and send patrol units swiftly to the scene, without having to wait for vague telephone reports from neighbors. In 1995 the Defense Department awarded a $1.7 million contract to Alliant Techsystems for its prototype system SECURES, which tests more advanced sound pickup networks in Washington and other cities. The hope is to distinguish not only types of gunfire but also human voices crying for help.

So far, so good. But from there, engineers say it would be simple to upgrade the equipment, enabling bored monitors to eavesdrop through open bedroom windows on cries of passion, or family arguments. "Of course we would never go that far," one official said, reassuringly.

Smaller and Cheaper

Consider another piece of James Bond apparatus now available to anyone with ready cash. Today, almost any electronics store will sell you night vision goggles using state-of-the-art infrared optics equal to those issued by the military, for less than the price of a video camera. AGEMA Systems, of Syracuse, New York, has sold several police departments imaging devices that can peer into houses from the street, discriminate the heat given off by indoor marijuana cultivators, and sometimes tell if a person inside moves from one room to the next. Military and civilian enhanced vision technologies now move in lockstep, as they have in the computer field for years.

In other words, even darkness no longer guarantees privacy.

Nor does your garden wall. In 1995, Admiral William A. Owens, then vice chairman of the Joint Chiefs of Staff, described a sensor system that he expected to be operational within a few years: a pilotless drone, equipped to provide airborne surveillance for soldiers in the field. While camera robots in the $1 million range have been flying in the military for some time, the new system will be extraordinarily cheap and simple. Instead of requiring a large support crew, it will be controlled by one semiskilled soldier and will fit in the palm of a hand. Minuscule and quiet, such remote-piloted vehicles, or RPVs, may flit among trees to survey threats near a rifle platoon. When mass-produced in huge quantities, unit prices will fall.

Can civilian models be far behind? No law or regulation will keep them from our cities for very long. The rich, the powerful, and figures of authority will have them, whether legally or surreptitiously. And the contraptions will become smaller, cheaper, and smarter with each passing year.

So much for the supposed privacy enjoyed by sunbathers in their own backyards.

Moreover, surveillance cameras are the tip of the metaphorical iceberg. Other entrancing and invasive innovations of the vaunted *information age* abound. Will a paper envelope protect the correspondence you send by old-fashioned surface mail when new-style scanners can trace the patterns of ink inside without ever breaking the seal?

Computer Spying

Let's say you correspond with others by e-mail and use a computerized encryption program to ensure that your messages are read only by the intended recipient. What good will all the ciphers and codes do, if some adversary has bought a "back door" password to your encoding program? Or if a wasp-sized camera drone flits into your room, sticks to the ceiling above your desk, inflates a bubble lens, and watches every keystroke that you type? . . .

In late 1997 it was revealed that Swiss police had secretly tracked the whereabouts of mobile phone users via a telephone company computer that records billions of movements per year. Swisscom was able to locate its mobile subscribers within a few hundred meters. This aided several police investigations. But civil libertarians expressed heated concern, especially since identical technology is used worldwide.

The same issues arise when we contemplate the proliferation of vast databases containing information about our lives, habits, tastes, and personal histories. . . . The cash register scanners in a million supermarkets, video stores, and pharmacies already pour forth a flood of statistical data about customers and their purchases, ready to be correlated. (Are you stocking up on hemorrhoid cream? Renting a daytime motel room? The database knows.) Corporations claim this information helps them serve us more efficiently. Critics respond that it gives big companies an unfair advantage, enabling them to know vastly more about us than we do about them. Soon, computers will hold all your financial and educational records, legal documents, and medical analyses that parse you all the way down to your genes. Any of this might be examined by strangers without your knowledge, or even against your stated will.

As with those streetlamp cameras, the choices we make regarding future information networks—how they will be controlled and who can access the data—will affect our own lives and those of our children and their descendants.

Mapping the Genetic Blueprint for Human Life

Zarir E. Karanjawala and Francis S. Collins

DNA is the chemical blueprint of the human body. Coiled within its double helix are 3 billion chemical codes on which genes are located—much like cities along an expressway. Genes determine the particular characteristics of a living creature, from weight and eye color to genetic disposition to a disease.

One of the premiere breakthroughs of the 1990s came in the field of gene therapy. Researchers continued to discover new genes and the role they played in disease. As a result, tests for the presence of genes that make people sick or susceptible to disease became more and more available. As the decade drew to a close, scientists, aided by money from the Human Genome Project, were mapping and identifying all of the estimated fifty thousand to one hundred thousand genes on human DNA.

In this selection Zarir E. Karanjawala, a professor at the Southern California School of Medicine, and Francis S. Collins, a doctor who works at the National Human Genome Research Institute and the National Institutes of Health, contend that fewer than 20 percent of patients receive appropriate genetic counseling because of a lack of physician training in this new field.

Excerpted from "Genetics in the Context of Medical Practice," by Zarir E. Karanjawala, *JAMA, The Journal of the American Medical Association*, November 4, 1998.

The Human Genome Project (HGP) is an international scientific effort to map and sequence [all of the estimated fifty thousand to one hundred thousand genes on human DNA]. Since its inception in the United States in [1990], as a joint effort by the National Institutes of Health (NIH) and Department of Energy (DOE), the HGP now includes contributions from genome centers in the United Kingdom, France, Canada, Germany, and Japan. In September 1998, the NIH and DOE announced an accelerated timetable for sequencing the genome, and the entire human sequence is expected to be completed by the end of [2003]. This information will benefit clinical medicine by enabling physicians to diagnose and treat [inherited] disorders more effectively.

Information from the HGP has accelerated the rate of gene discovery. Once a disease gene is identified, DNA-based diagnostic tests can be developed to detect at-risk individuals. Knowledge of a patient's genetic makeup can allow physicians to minimize disease risk through preventive medicine and conventional drug [therapies]. A more novel treatment is gene therapy, which compensates for the defective gene by providing [a] . . . functional copy. Another promising tool is pharmacogenomics, where a person's genotype is used to predict those [drug treatments] that will prove most therapeutic and identify those that could be [harmful]. . . .

Physicians Need to Update Knowledge of Genetics

As discoveries from the HGP are translated into meaningful medical diagnostics and therapeutics, genetics will heavily influence clinical decision making. As the number of treatable genetic diseases increases, physicians will need to use and interpret genetic tests correctly, determine those genetic treatments that are available, and learn how to access these services. Perhaps the most important role for the primary care physician is first to identify a potential genetic disorder. Hence, physicians must be prepared to integrate information derived from a careful family history with the molecular data provided by the HGP.

A recent American Medical Association (AMA) survey indicated that 59% of Americans are somewhat or very likely to take advantage of genetic testing and that 72% believe that their primary care physician can interpret these [results]. However, in a recent study, physicians misinterpreted nearly one third of predictive test results for colon cancer, and fewer than 20% of patients received appropriate genetic [counseling].

To strengthen genetics knowledge among physicians, recent guidelines by the American Society of Human Genetics have concentrated on increasing the emphasis on genetics in medical school [curricula]. To ensure quality continuing genetics education for health care professionals, the National Coalition for Health Professional Education in Genetics was developed in 1996 . . . to provide genetics information online, better represent genetics on licensing examinations, and facilitate the development of core curricula in [genetics]. . . .

Protecting Patient Rights

A recent survey indicated that nearly 7 out of 10 Americans are somewhat or very concerned that genetic information may be used against them by either their employer or health insurance [provider]. In 1995, a set of recommendations to lawmakers dealing with issues pertaining to health insurance and genetic discrimination was compiled by the NIH-DOE Working Group on Ethical, Legal and Social Implications of Human Genome Research and the National Action Plan on Breast [Cancer]. These guidelines would prohibit insurance providers from increasing premiums or determining eligibility based on predictive genetic information and would prohibit insurance providers from accessing or disclosing genetic information. A major step in this direction came in 1996 with passage of the Health Insurance Portability and Accountability Act (HIPAA), which prevents establishing in group health plans differential premiums based on genetic status and does not consider genetic information a "pre-existing" [condition]. Unfortunately, the HIPAA does not ensure the privacy of genetic information, nor does it protect those insured in the individual market. Several active efforts are under way at the federal level to address these problems. The Patients' Bill of Rights Act, introduced by Republican members of the Senate in July 1998, would extend protection to those seeking

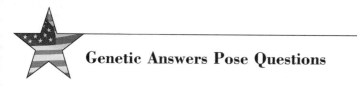

Genetic Answers Pose Questions

As the 1990s drew to a close, genetic research began to answer age-old questions about heredity and disease. But, as this excerpt printed in the Economist *shows, the new technology posed many new moral and ethical questions regarding everything from possible genetic weapons to criminal law.*

As happened with the description of atomic particles, [the mapping of human genes] opens up frightening possibilities and ethical dilemmas. Can new forms of life be created? If life can be mapped, can it be replicated? Might genetic weapons be made to spread diseases, either known or newly created? If a genetic basis can be described for criminal behaviour might criminals come to be seen as victims of their genes rather than violators of the law? Might individuals carrying such genes be persecuted even if they had done no wrong? If scientists can identify the genetic basis for height or brainpower, might parents be able to specify their children's height or intelligence? Can parents "choose" their children?

All those questions are for the future—some for a distant one. Meanwhile, there is one last thing that makes the Human Genome Project unlike any other big science project so far. It will lead to discoveries that will make some people a lot of money. And because of that, as well as because the thirst for knowledge seems unstoppable, the genome project seems certain to continue to its end—wherever that may be.

Economist, "The Human Genome," September 14, 1996.

individual insurance coverage by preventing the use of predictive genetic information to deny [coverage]. It would also protect policy holders and applicants from being forced to take genetic tests or provide the results of previous tests, and extends the definition of genetic information to include family history in addition to test results. While the status of this legislation is uncertain, it is clear that patients need to be protected from potential genetic discrimination and stigmatization, in both the health insurance and employment arenas.

Genetic technologies are increasingly relevant to both the diagnosis and therapy of human disease. If patients are to benefit from this knowledge, clinicians will need to incorporate genetic medicine into clinical practice much like any other aspect of the classic history and physical examination. Public interest in genetic advances, coupled with an explosion of information provided by the HGP, will place the primary care physician in a central role to deliver genetic discoveries to the patient's bedside. This truly is an exciting time to be practicing medicine.

Scientists Rush to Utilize Cloning

Elizabeth Pennisi

In 1997 researchers in Edinburgh, Scotland, cloned a lamb named Dolly from a single cell of an adult sheep. This was a major advancement in reproduction technology. But it was startling as well. Unlike normal offspring, Dolly was an exact copy of her mother—her identical twin.

In the opinion of Elizabeth Pennisi, a staff writer at *Science* magazine, cloning could become a useful tool. Farmers could clone their prize-winning cows to produce more milk from smaller herds, and cloning could be useful in medicine to regenerate damaged tissue and grow organs on animal donors.

Births are usually announced on a newspaper's society or personal pages, not on the front page. But that convention didn't apply to Dolly and Polly and—[in January 1998]—George and Charlie. These white-faced lambs and Holstein calves made headlines as the products of cloning technologies that have generated fascination and fear—a reaction fanned . . . by the improbable claims of a physicist who says he plans to clone adult humans [by the year 2000]. But the technologies have done more than spawn an ethical debate about the prospects for human cloning: They have also galvanized efforts to create [cloned or] transgenic livestock that will act as living factories, producing pharmaceutical products in their milk for treating human diseases and, perhaps, organs for transplantation.

That was always the main intention of Dolly's creators, Ian Wilmut, Keith Campbell, and their colleagues at the Roslin Institute and PPL Therapeutics in Roslin, Scotland. But in the year since the announcement of Dolly's birth, a dozen other groups have been adapting the technique used by the team in Scotland. Some want to clone animals bearing working copies of transplanted genes. Although key problems remain to be solved, these efforts . . . have already resulted in the birth of sheep containing a human clotting factor gene and calves containing foreign marker genes.

Experiments in which the nuclei of pig cells have been fused with cow eggs have also given tantalizing results. This work is invigorating the "pharming" industry: Underwriting the cloning frenzy are biotech and pharmaceutical companies eager to cash in on its potential for creating transgenic livestock. "There is a huge industry that is organizing itself around [the new cloning] technology," says James Robl, a developmental biologist of the University of Massachusetts, Amherst.

An Efficient Way to Produce Clones

There is, however, a crucial difference between these experiments and the original Dolly breakthrough—a distinction that has sometimes been lost in the public discussion of the implications of these new results. Dolly was cloned by taking nuclei from adult mammary gland cells, starving them of nutrients to reset their cell cycles, then fusing them with sheep eggs whose own nuclei had been removed. But this procedure was very inefficient—producing only one success out of the 277 eggs that took up the new DNA. The later experiments all use nuclei from fetal cells, which have proved more efficient at generating viable offspring than adult cells. Indeed, so far the Dolly experiment has not been exactly replicated, and some scientists have even questioned whether Dolly is in fact the clone of an adult.

Animal geneticists have jumped on the technology because it potentially offers a far more efficient way to pro-

The successful cloning of a lamb in Scotland has opened up new possibilities for, as well as fears about, the use of cloning technology in farming and medicine.

duce transgenic animals than previous techniques, which involve the injection of foreign DNA into newly fertilized eggs. The success of an egg injection is not known until after the offspring is born. For example, using egg injection, PPL Therapeutics took years to develop a flock of 600 transgenic sheep, as only about 4% of the lambs carried the desired gene.

In contrast, nuclear transfer technology allows researchers to select as nucleus donors only those cells that express the transplanted gene. Moreover, in theory, those cells could provide as many clones as needed in a single generation. "In one fell swoop, you get what you want," says PPL research director Alan Colman. Indeed, Will Eyestone of PPL's Blacksburg, Virginia, facility [claimed] . . . that egg injection "may well become old-fashioned."

Farming Human Proteins

Campbell, who recently moved from the Roslin Institute to PPL's labs 300 meters down the road, Wilmut, and their colleagues were the first to announce that they had been able to produce transgenic animals with cloning technology. They reported in December that they had produced three clone sheep, two of which are still alive, carrying the human . . . clotting protein.

Now, Advanced Cell Technology has achieved in cows what the team in Scotland did with sheep: Robl and his colleague Steven Stice announced . . . the birth of two [cloned] calves . . . George and Charlie . . . born in mid-January 1998. A third has been born since the announcement, and more are on the way. "[They are] the first transgenic cloned calves, and that's great," says Campbell of PPL, which is also doing nuclear transfer work in cattle. . . .

That demonstration has been eagerly awaited. Transgenic cows, which produce 9,000 liters of milk per year, should be better factories for therapeutic proteins than sheep or goats. "Milk is cheap, and we have an incredible dairy infrastructure," points out Carol Ziomek, an embryologist with Genzyme Transgenics in Framingham, Massachusetts.

Indeed, that potential has already spurred a gold rush. In October 1997, Genzyme Transgenics awarded Advanced Cell Technology a 5 year, $10 million contract to develop transgenic cows that will produce albumin, a human blood protein used in fluids for treating people who have suffered large blood losses. And [in January 1998], Pharming Holding N.V. in Leiden, the Netherlands, formed an alliance with ABS Global, an animal breeding company in DeForest, Wisconsin, and its spin-off company, Infigen Inc., to develop transgenic cattle that produce . . . human blood proteins . . . in their milk.

Other efforts are aimed at expanding the utility of pigs, particularly in biomedicine. A few companies and research groups hope to use pig organs or tissue to help meet the large unfilled demand for transplant organs. The goal is to genetically modify the animals' tissues so they are less readily rejected [by the human body]. Also, because a pig's physiology is more like a human's than is a mouse's, some animal scientists argue that pigs could be good models for studying human diseases if their genetic makeup could be modified so that they develop appropriate symptoms. . . .

The Drawbacks of Cloning

In spite of the rapid advances in nuclear transfer since Dolly's debut, some big obstacles still remain. At each step along the way some—often many—individuals don't survive. That low efficiency doomed an earlier version of nuclear transfer when it made its commercial debut [in the 1980s]. At that time, several companies, including Granada Inc., based in Houston, were going great guns using nuclei from very early embryos to clone hundreds of calves to make large herds of genetically superior beef cattle. But by 1991, Granada had shut its doors. "We couldn't make as many calves as we wanted to," recalls [Alexion] Bondioli, who worked there. And too often, calves were oversized and unhealthy, with lungs that were not fully developed at birth.

Researchers see the same trends in the few cows and sheep produced by the newer cloning procedures. Large numbers of deaths occur around the time of birth. For example, PPL and Roslin lost eight of eleven lambs in their first experiment with transgenic clones. But it's not the nuclear transfer procedure itself that's at fault, says Robl. Animals produced by in vitro fertilization and other procedures involving the manipulation of embryos have similar problems, albeit at a lower frequency.

"Something that you do to the embryo . . . leads to a problem nine months later," says George Seidel Jr., a physiologist at Colorado State University in Fort Collins. His data and other observations suggest that in problem calves the placenta does not function as it should. As a result, cloned calves have too little oxygen and low concentrations of certain growth factors in their blood.

While some researchers are experimenting with different nutrient solutions or making other subtle changes in their nuclear transfer techniques to make embryos and newborns thrive, others are frantically trying to hone the genetic manipulation techniques. Researchers currently have no control over where the foreign genes end up in the chromosomes or how many copies of the gene become part of that cell's genetic repertoire.

Developing that control would enable them to knock out specific genes, say the one encoding the pig protein that elicits a strong, immediate rejection response to pig organ transplants. "The Holy Grail for many is finding a way of getting targeted disruption of genes in livestock as we have in mice," explains Colman, who is confident that even this tough molecular biology problem will be solved quickly. "I expect we'll have targeting solved by [1999]," he predicts.

Such confidence is required in this fast-moving field, in which progress generally comes through trial and error. Understanding how it all works, say these scientists, will come later. "[There] clearly is at this point in time a pushing forward of the technology," says . . . Bondioli. "Have we learned any more biology? Probably not. But [we] have opened up a means to study [it]."

The Brave New World of Biotechnology

Jeremy Rifkin

At the dawn of the twenty-first century, amazing scientific discoveries in genetics and technology allowed scientists to begin making revolutionary changes in the way humans grew food, reproduced, and cured disease. According to Jeremy Rifkin, the author of fourteen books on economic trends and matters relating to science, technology, and culture, the new genetic commerce raised troubling questions as the "bioindustry" began to dominate farming and medicine. Would parents some day be able to chose the physical traits and intelligence of their future offspring? Would genetically engineered sources of food and fiber forever change the agricultural era that had lasted since the beginning of civilization?

Never before in history has humanity been so unprepared for the new technological and economic opportunities, challenges, and risks that lie on the horizon. Our way of life is likely to be more fundamentally transformed in the next several decades than in the previous one thousand years. By the year 2025, we and our children may be living in a world utterly different from anything human beings have ever experienced in the past.

In little more than a generation, our definition of life and

---

the meaning of existence is likely to be radically altered. Long-held assumptions about nature, including our own human nature, are likely to be rethought. Many age-old practices regarding sexuality, reproduction, birth, and parenthood could be partially abandoned. Ideas about equality and democracy are also likely to be redefined, as well as our vision of what is meant by terms such as "free will" and "progress." Our very sense of self and society will likely change, as it did when the early Renaissance spirit swept over medieval Europe more than seven hundred years ago.

There are many convergent forces coming together to create this powerful new social current. At the epicenter is a technology revolution unmatched in all of history in its power to remake ourselves, our institutions, and our world. Scientists are beginning to reorganize life at the genetic level. The new tools of biology are opening up opportunities for refashioning life on Earth while foreclosing options that have existed over the millennia of evolutionary history. Before our eyes lies an uncharted new landscape whose contours are being shaped in thousands of biotechnology laboratories in universities, government agencies, and corporations around the world. If the claims already being made for the new science are only partially realized, the consequences for society and future generations are likely to be enormous. . . .

The Bioindustrial World

A handful of global corporations, research institutions, and governments could hold patents on virtually all 100,000 genes that make up the blueprints of the human race, as well as the cells, organs, and tissues that comprise the human body. They may also own similar patents on tens of thousands of micro-organisms, plants, and animals, allowing them unprecedented power to dictate the terms by which we and future generations will live our lives.

Global agriculture could find itself in the midst of a great transition in world history, with an increasing volume of food and fiber being grown indoors in tissue culture in giant bacteria baths, at a fraction of the price of growing staples on the land. The shift to indoor agriculture could presage the eventual elimination of the agricultural era that stretched from the neolithic revolution some ten thousand years ago, to the green revolution of the latter half of the twentieth century. While indoor agriculture could mean cheaper prices and a more abundant supply of food, millions of farmers in both the developing and developed world could be uprooted from the land, sparking one of the great social upheavals in world history.

Tens of thousands of novel transgenic bacteria, viruses, plants and animals could be released into the Earth's ecosystems for commercial tasks ranging from "bio-remediation" to the production of alternative fuels. Some of those releases, however, could wreak havoc with the planet's biosphere, spreading destabilizing and even deadly generic pollution across the world. Military uses of the new technology might have equally devastating effects on the Earth and its inhabitants. Genetically engineered biological warfare agents could pose as serious a threat to global security in the coming century as nuclear weapons do now.

Experiments in biotechnology will someday produce more food at cheaper prices, but may have unknown health or environmental risks.

Animal and human cloning could be commonplace, with "replication" partially replacing "reproduction" for the first time in history. Genetically customized and mass-produced animal clones could be used as chemical factories to secrete—in their blood and milk—large volumes of inexpensive chemicals and drugs for human use. We could also see the creation of a range of new chimeric animals on Earth, including human/animal hybrids. A chimp/hume, half chimpanzee and half human, for example, could become a reality. The human/animal hybrids could be widely used as experimental subjects in medical research and as organ "donors" for xenotransplantation. The artificial creation and propagation of cloned, chimeric, and transgenic animals could mean the end of the wild and the substitution of a bioindustrial world.

Some parents might choose to have their children conceived in test tubes and gestated in artificial wombs outside the human body to avoid the unpleasantries of pregnancy and to ensure a safe, transparent environment through which to monitor their unborn child's development. Genetic changes could be made in human fetuses in the womb to correct deadly diseases and disorders and to enhance mood, behavior, intelligence, and physical traits. Parents might be able to design some of the characteristics of their own children, fundamentally altering the very notion of parenthood. "Customized" babies could pave the way for the rise of a eugenic civilization in the twenty-first century.

Millions of people could obtain a detailed genetic readout of themselves, allowing them to gaze into their own biological futures. The genetic information would give people the power to predict and plan their lives in ways never before possible. That same "genetic information," however, could be used by schools, employers, insurance companies, and governments to determine educational tracks, employment prospects, insurance premiums, and security clearances, giving rise to a new and virulent form of discrimination based on one's genetic profile. Our notions of sociality and equity could be transformed. Meritocracy could give way to genetocracy, with individuals, ethnic groups, and races increasingly categorized and stereotyped by genotype, making way for the emergence of an informal biological caste system in countries around the world.

The Biotech Century could bring some or even most of these changes and many more into our daily lives, deeply affecting our individual and collective consciousness, the future of our civilization, and the biosphere itself. The benefits and perils of what some are calling "the ultimate technology frontier" are both exciting to behold and chilling to contemplate. Still, despite both the formidable potential and ominous nature of this extraordinary technology revolution, until now far more public attention has been focused on the other great technology revolution of the twenty-first century—computers and telecommunications. That's about to change. After more than forty years of running on parallel tracks, the information and life sciences are slowly beginning to fuse into a single technological and economic force. The computer is increasingly being used to decipher, manage, and organize the vast genetic information that is the raw resource of the emerging biotech economy. Scientists working in the new field of "bioinformatics" are beginning to download the genetic information of millions of years of evolution, creating a powerful new genre of "biological data banks." The rich genetic information in these biological data banks is being used by researchers to remake the natural world.

The marriage of computers and genes forever alters our reality at the deepest levels of human experience. To begin to comprehend the enormity of the shift taking place in human civilization, it's important to step back and gain a better understanding of the historic nature of the many changes that are occurring around us as we turn the corner into a new century. Those changes represent a turning point for civilization. We are in the throes of one of the great transformations in world history. Before us lies the passing of one great economic era and the birth pains of another. As the past is always prelude to the future, our journey into the Biotech Century needs to begin with an account of the world we're leaving behind. . . .

A New Economic Era

Great economic changes in history occur when a number of technological and social forces come together to create a new "operating matrix." There are seven strands that make up the operational matrix of the Biotech Century. Together, they create a framework for a new economic era.

First, the ability to isolate, identify, and recombine genes is making the gene pool available, for the first time, as the primary raw resource for future economic activity. Recombinant DNA techniques and other biotechnologies allow scientists and biotech companies to locate, manipulate, and exploit genetic resources for specific economic ends.

Second, the awarding of patents on genes, cell lines, genetically engineered tissue, organs, and organisms, as well as the processes used to alter them, is giving the marketplace the commercial incentive to exploit the new resources.

Third, the globalization of commerce and trade make possible the wholesale reseeding of the Earth's biosphere with a laboratory-conceived second Genesis, an artificially produced bioindustrial nature designed to replace nature's own evolutionary scheme. A global life-science industry is already beginning to wield unprecedented power over the vast biological resources of the planet. Life-science fields ranging from agriculture to medicine are being consolidated under the umbrella of giant "life" companies in the emerging biotech marketplace.

Fourth, the mapping of the approximately 100,000 genes that comprise the human genome, new breakthroughs in genetic screening, including DNA chips, somatic gene therapy, and the imminent prospect of genetic engineering of human eggs, sperm, and embryonic cells, is paving the way for the wholesale alteration of the human species and the birth of a commercially driven eugenics civilization.

Fifth, a spate of new scientific studies on the genetic basis of human behavior and the new sociobiology that favors nature over nurture are providing a cultural context for the widespread acceptance of the new biotechnologies.

Sixth, the computer is providing the communication and organizational medium to manage the genetic information that makes up the biotech economy. All over the world, researchers are using computers to decipher, download, catalogue, and organize genetic information, creating a new store of genetic capital for use in the bioindustrial age.

Computational technologies and genetic technologies are fusing together into a powerful new technological reality.

Seventh, a new cosmological narrative about evolution is beginning to challenge the neo-Darwinian citadel with a view of nature that is compatible with the operating assumptions of the new technologies and the new global economy. The new ideas about nature provide the legitimizing framework for the Biotech Century by suggesting that the new way we are reorganizing our economy and society are amplifications of nature's own principles and practices and, therefore, justifiable.

The Biotech Century brings with it a new resource base, a new set of transforming technologies, new forms of commercial protection to spur commerce, a global trading market to reseed the Earth with an artificial second Genesis, an emerging eugenics science, a new supporting sociology, a new communication tool to organize and manage economic activity at the genetic level, and a new cosmological narrative to accompany the journey. Together, genes, biotechnologies, life patents, the global life-science industry, human-gene screening and surgery, the new cultural currents, computers, and the revised theories of evolution are beginning to remake our world.

Environmental Concerns

Al Gore

On April 22, 1990, Earth Day celebrated its twentieth anniversary—claiming 200 million participants worldwide who gathered together to celebrate the ecology movement. Throughout the nineties, Americans continued to celebrate Earth Day. But in this selection, Vice President Al Gore contends that humankind's effects on the earth continued to cause environmental problems.

Although it was impossible for scientists in the 1990s to predict the outcome of humankind's impact on the earth, Gore, along with a majority of Americans, voiced many concerns about the environment. In *Earth in the Balance,* written when he was still a senator, Gore urged people to rethink their relationship with nature to help preserve the earth's ecology for future generations.

Al Gore is the descendent of a long American political dynasty who was a Democratic senator from Tennessee and served as Bill Clinton's vice president from 1992 to 2000.

I was standing in the sun on the hot steel deck of a fishing ship capable of processing a fifty-ton catch on a good day. But it wasn't a good day. We were anchored in what used to be the most productive fishing site in all of central Asia, but as I looked out over the bow, the prospects of a good catch looked bleak. Where there should have been gentle blue-green waves lapping against the side of the ship, there was nothing but hot dry sand—as far as I could see in all directions. The other ships of the fleet were also at rest in the sand, scattered in the dunes that stretched all the way to the horizon. . . .

As a camel walked by on the dead bottom of the Aral Sea, my thoughts returned to the unlikely ship of the desert on which I stood, which also seemed to be illustrating the point that its world had changed out from underneath it with sudden cruelty. Ten years ago the Aral was the fourth-largest inland sea in the world, comparable to the largest of North America's Great Lakes. Now it is disappearing because the water that used to feed it has been diverted in an ill-considered irrigation scheme to grow cotton in the desert. The new shoreline was almost forty kilometers across the sand from where the fishing fleet was now permanently docked. Meanwhile, in the nearby town of Muynak the people were still canning fish—brought not from the Aral Sea but shipped by rail through Siberia from the Pacific Ocean, more than a thousand miles away.

I had come to the Aral Sea in August 1990 to witness at first hand the destruction taking place there on an almost biblical scale. But during the trip I encountered other images that also alarmed me. For example, the day I returned to Moscow from Muynak, my friend Alexei Yablokov, possibly the leading environmentalist in the Soviet Union, was returning from an emergency expedition to the White Sea, where he had investigated the mysterious and unprecedented death of several *million* starfish, washed up into a knee-deep mass covering many miles of beach. That night, in his apartment, he talked of what it was like for the residents to wade through the starfish in hip boots, trying to explain their death.

An Unfamiliar Tide Rising

Later investigations identified radioactive military waste as the likely culprit in the White Sea deaths. But what about all of the other mysterious mass deaths washing up on beaches around the world? French scientists recently concluded that the explanation for the growing number of dead dolphins washing up along the Riviera was accumulated environmental stress, which, over time, rendered the animals too weak to fight off a virus. This same phenomenon may also explain the sudden increase in dolphin deaths along the Gulf Coast in Texas as well as the mysterious deaths of 12,000 seals whose corpses washed up on the shores of the North Sea in the summer of 1988. Of course, the oil-covered otters and seabirds of Prince William Sound a year later presented less of a mystery to science, if no less an indictment of our civilization.

As soon as one of these troubling images fades, another takes its place, provoking new questions. What does it mean, for example, that children playing in the morning surf must now dodge not only the occasional jellyfish but the occasional hypodermic needle washing in with the waves? Needles, dead dolphins, and oil-soaked birds—are all these signs that the shores of our familiar world are fast eroding, that we are now standing on some new beach, facing dangers beyond the edge of what we are capable of imagining?

With our backs turned to the place in nature from which we came, we sense an unfamiliar tide rising and swirling around our ankles, pulling at the sand beneath our feet. Each time this strange new tide goes out, it leaves behind the flotsam and jetsam of some giant shipwreck far out at sea, startling images washed up on the sands of our time, each a fresh warning of hidden dangers that lie ahead if we continue on our present course.

My search for the underlying causes of the environmental crisis has led me to travel around the world to examine and study many of these images of destruction. At the very bottom of the earth, high in the Trans-Antarctic Mountains, with the sun glaring at midnight through a hole in the sky, I stood in the unbelievable coldness and talked with a scientist in the late fall of 1988 about the tunnel he was digging through time. Slipping his parka back to reveal

184

a badly burned face that was cracked and peeling, he pointed to the annual layers of ice in a core sample dug from the glacier on which we were standing. He moved his finger back in time to the ice of two decades ago. "Here's where the U.S. Congress passed the Clean Air Act," he said. At the bottom of the world, two continents away from Washington, D.C., even a small reduction in one country's emissions had changed the amount of pollution found in the remotest and least accessible place on earth.

Burning Coal and Oil

But the most significant change thus far in the earth's atmosphere is the one that began with the industrial revolution early in the nineteenth century and has picked up speed ever since. Industry meant coal, and later oil, and we began to burn lots of it—bringing rising levels of carbon dioxide (CO_2), with its ability to trap more heat in the atmosphere and slowly warm the earth. Fewer than a hundred yards from the South Pole, upwind from the ice runway where the ski plane lands and keeps its engines running to prevent the metal parts from freeze-locking together, scientists monitor the air several times every day to chart the course of that inexorable change. During my visit, I watched one scientist draw the results of that day's measurements, pushing the end of a steep line still higher on the graph. He told me how easy it is—there at the end of the earth—to see that this enormous change in the global atmosphere is still picking up speed.

Two and a half years later I slept under the midnight sun at the other end of our planet, in a small tent pitched on a twelve-foot-thick slab of ice floating in the frigid Arctic Ocean. After a hearty breakfast, my companions and I traveled by snowmobiles a few miles farther north to a rendezvous point where the ice was thinner—only three and a half feet thick—and a nuclear submarine hovered in the water below. After it crashed through the ice, took on its new passengers, and resubmerged, I talked with scientists who were trying to measure more accurately the thickness of the polar ice cap, which many believe is thinning as a result of global warming. I had just negotiated an agreement between ice scientists and the U.S. Navy to secure the release of previously top secret data from submarine sonar tracks, data that could help them learn what is happening to the north polar cap. Now, I wanted to see the pole itself, and some eight hours after we met the submarine, we were crashing through that ice, surfacing, and then I was standing in an eerily beautiful snowscape, windswept and sparkling white, with the horizon defined by little hummocks, or "pressure ridges" of ice that are pushed up like tiny mountain ranges when separate sheets collide. But here too, CO_2 levels are rising just as rapidly, and ultimately temperatures will rise with them—indeed, global warming is expected to push temperatures up much more rapidly in the polar regions than in the rest of the world. As the polar air warms, the ice here will thin; and since the polar cap plays such a crucial role in the world's weather system, the consequences of a thinning cap could be disastrous.

Considering such scenarios is not a purely speculative exercise. Six months after I returned from the North Pole, a team of scientists reported dramatic changes in the pattern of ice distribution in the Arctic, and a second team reported a still controversial claim (which a variety of data now suggest) that, overall, the north polar cap has thinned by 2 percent in just the 1980s. Moreover, scientists established . . . that in many land areas north of the Arctic Circle, the spring snowmelt now comes earlier every year, and deep in the tundra below, the temperature of the earth is steadily rising.

Rain Forests and Coral Reefs

As it happens, some of the most disturbing images of environmental destruction can be found exactly halfway between the North and South poles—precisely at the equator in Brazil—where billowing clouds of smoke regularly blacken the sky above the immense but now threatened Amazon rain forest. Acre by acre, the rain forest is being burned to create fast pasture for fast-food beef; as I learned when I went there in early 1989, the fires are set earlier and earlier in the dry season now, with more than one Tennessee's worth of rain forest being slashed and burned each year. According to our guide, the biologist Tom Lovejoy, there are more different species of birds in each square mile of the Amazon than exist in all of North America—which means we are silencing thousands of songs we have never even heard.

But for most of us the Amazon is a distant place, and we scarcely notice the disappearance of these and other vulnerable species. We ignore these losses at our peril, however. They're like the proverbial miners' canaries, silent alarms whose message in this case is that living species of animals and plants are now vanishing around the world *one thousand times faster* than at any time in the past 65 million years.

To be sure, the deaths of some of the larger and more spectacular animal species now under siege do occasionally capture our attention. I have also visited another place along the equator, East Africa, where I encountered the grotesquely horrible image of a dead elephant, its head mutilated by poachers who had dug out its valuable tusks with chain saws. Clearly, we need to change our purely aesthetic consideration of ivory, since its source is now so threatened. To me, its translucent whiteness seems different now, like evidence of the ghostly presence of a troubled spirit, a beautiful but chill apparition, inspiring both wonder and dread.

A similar apparition lies just beneath the ocean. While scuba diving in the Caribbean, I have seen and touched the white bones of a dead coral reef. All over the earth, coral reefs have suddenly started to "bleach" as warmer ocean temperatures put unaccustomed stress on the tiny organisms that normally live in the skin of the coral and give the reef its natural coloration. As these organisms—nicknamed "zooks"—leave the membrane of the coral, the coral itself becomes transparent, allowing its white limestone skeleton to shine through—hence its bleached appearance. In the past, bleaching was almost always an occasional and temporary phenomenon, but repeated episodes can exhaust the coral. In the last few years, scientists have been shocked at the sudden occurrence of extensive worldwide bleaching episodes from which increasing numbers of coral reefs have failed to recover. Though dead, they shine more brightly than before, haunted perhaps by the same ghost that gives spectral light to an elephant's tusk.

Woodlands into Concrete

But one doesn't have to travel around the world to witness humankind's assault on the earth. Images that signal the distress of our global environment are now commonly seen almost anywhere. A few miles from the Capitol, for example, I encountered another startling image of nature out of place. Driving in the Arlington, Virginia, neighborhood where my family and I live when the Senate is in session, I stepped on the brake to avoid hitting a large pheasant walking across the street. It darted between the parked cars, across the sidewalk, and into a neighbor's backyard. Then it was gone. But this apparition of wildness persisted in my memory as a puzzle: Why would a pheasant, let alone such a large and beautiful mature specimen, be out for a walk in my neighborhood? Was it a much wilder place than I had noticed? Were pheasants, like the trendy Vietnamese potbellied pigs, becoming the latest fashion in unusual pets? I didn't solve the mystery until weeks later, when I remembered that about three miles away, along the edge of the river, developers were bulldozing the last hundred acres of untouched forest in the entire area. As the woods fell to make way for more concrete, more buildings, parking lots, and streets, the wild things that lived there were forced to flee. Most of the deer were hit by cars; other creatures—like the pheasant that darted into my neighbor's backyard—made it a little farther.

Ironically, before I understood the mystery, I felt vaguely comforted to imagine that perhaps this urban environment, so similar to the one in which many Americans live, was not so hostile to wild things after all. I briefly supposed that, like the resourceful raccoons and possums and squirrels and pigeons, all of whom have adapted to life in the suburbs, creatures as wild as pheasants might have a fighting chance. Now I remember that pheasant when I take my children to the zoo and see an elephant or a rhinoceros. They too inspire wonder and sadness. They too remind me that we are creating a world that is hostile to wildness, that seems to prefer concrete to natural landscapes. We are encountering these creatures on a path we have paved—one that ultimately leads to their extinction.

Clouds of Methane

On some nights, in high northern latitudes, the sky itself offers another ghostly image that signals the loss of ecological balance now in progress. If the sky is clear after sunset—and if you are watching from a place where pollution hasn't blotted out the night sky altogether—you can sometimes see a strange kind of cloud high in the sky. This "noctilucent cloud" occasionally appears when the earth is first cloaked in the evening darkness; shimmering above us with a translucent whiteness, these clouds seem quite unnatural. And they should: noctilucent clouds have begun to appear more often because of a huge buildup of methane gas in the atmosphere. (Also called natural gas, methane is released from landfills, from coal mines and rice paddies, from billions of termites that swarm through the freshly cut forestland, from the burning of biomass and from a variety of other human activities.) Even though noctilucent clouds were sometimes seen in the past, all this extra methane carries more water vapor into the upper atmosphere, where it condenses at much higher altitudes to form more clouds that the sun's rays still strike long after sunset has brought the beginning of night to the surface far beneath them.

What should we feel toward these ghosts in the sky? Simple wonder or the mix of emotions we feel at the zoo? Perhaps we should feel awe for our own power: just as men tear tusks from elephants' heads in such quantity as to

189

threaten the beast with extinction, we are ripping matter from its place in the earth in such volume as to upset the balance between daylight and darkness. In the process, we are once again adding to the threat of global warming, because methane has been one of the fastest-growing greenhouse gases, and is third only to carbon dioxide and water vapor in total volume, changing the chemistry of the upper atmosphere. But, without even considering that threat, shouldn't it startle us that we have now put these clouds in the evening sky which glisten with a spectral light? Or have our eyes adjusted so completely to the bright lights of civilization that we can't see these clouds for what they are— a physical manifestation of the violent collision between human civilization and the earth?

Chronology

1990
February 4—Mass rallies and strikes are held in Moscow to protest Communist rule in the Soviet Union.

August 2—Iraqi troops, on the orders of President Saddam Hussein, invade the small, oil-rich Arab country of Kuwait.

August 16—In a mission called Operation Desert Shield, tens of thousands of U.S. soldiers arrive in Saudi Arabia preparing to fight Iraq to regain Kuwait's independence.

October—President George Bush reneges on his campaign pledge and raises taxes.

1991
January 16—An international coalition of allied air forces led by the United States begins massive bombing raids on Iraq to begin Operation Desert Storm.

February 28—The Gulf War officially ends; Kuwait's independence is restored, but Saddam Hussein remains president of Iraq.

June 6—Boris Yeltsin is elected president of the Russian Republic.

August 19—Soviet general secretary Mikhail Gorbachev is briefly overthrown by Communist hard-liners.

October 15—Clarence Thomas is confirmed as a justice on the U.S. Supreme Court.

August 29—The Soviet legislature suspends all activities of the Communist Party; this is the first time in seventy years that the USSR is not ruled by Communists.

December 25—Gorbachev resigns and transfers power to Yeltsin; the Soviet Union is dissolved and replaced by a commonwealth of independent states.

1992
April 29—The verdict in the Rodney King case ignites riots in Los Angeles.

June 28—The biggest earthquake in forty years, measuring 7.4

on the Richter scale, rocks southern California.

August—Ethnic cleansing begins in Bosnia-Herzegovina as Serbia begins a campaign of terror and genocide against Muslims.

August 21—Federal agents engage Randall Weaver, his friend, and family in a shootout at Ruby Ridge, Idaho, killing Weaver's wife and his fourteen-year-old son.

November 2—Bill Clinton and Al Gore win the national presidential race.

December 9—U.S. troops land in Somalia to deliver humanitarian aid.

1993

February 11—Janet Reno becomes the first female attorney general of the United States.

February 26—The World Trade Center is bombed by four men associated with radical Middle Eastern terrorist groups.

February 28—The Bureau of Alcohol, Tobacco, and Firearms attempts to serve a warrant on the Branch Davidian compound in Waco, Texas; the resulting shootout kills six federal agents and wounds sixteen while six Branch Davidians are killed.

April 19—The standoff with the Branch Davidians in Waco ends with a firestorm that kills more than eighty people.

1994

January—The Justice Department subpoenas files pertaining to the Clintons' Whitewater investments, starting an investigation that lasts more than four years; discoveries made during the investigation eventually lead to Clinton's impeachment.

January 17—A major earthquake measuring 6.6 on the Richter scale hits Los Angeles, killing fifty-five people.

February—NATO begins its first offensive in Bosnia when U.S. jet fighters shoot down four Serbian jets.

September 27—Some 350 Republican candidates gather on the steps of the Capitol building to sign the Contract with America.

November 8—In midterm elections, Republicans gain a majority in the House and Senate for the first time in over forty years.

1995

April 19—Timothy McVeigh ignites a truck bomb in front of the Alfred Murrah Building in Oklahoma City, killing 168 people.

September—The *New York Times* and the *Washington Post* jointly print the Unabomber's manifesto.

December 14—The presidents of Bosnia, Croatia, and Serbia sign a peace accord in Paris.

1996

August 22—President Clinton signs the Personal Responsibility and Work Opportunity Act, which changes welfare rules for 13 million Americans.

November—Clinton becomes the first Democrat to get reelected as president since 1944; the Republican Congress is first to get reelected since 1930.

1997

President Clinton announces a plan to link every U.S. classroom to the Internet by the year 2000.

April—Researchers in Scotland clone a lamb named Dolly from a single cell of an adult sheep.

June 2—Timothy McVeigh is convicted on eleven counts of murder and conspiracy in relation to the Oklahoma City bombing; he is sentenced to die by lethal injection.

Summer—The Lilith Fair grosses $16 million in thirty-eight shows with an all-female roster of rock musicians; the all-women show is a first.

August 31—Diana, princess of Wales, dies in a car accident in a Paris tunnel.

October 2—Luke Woodham, age sixteen, stabs his mother to death, then goes to school and shoots nine of his classmates, killing two of them; this starts a gruesome trend of schoolyard killings.

1998

May—Theodore J. Kaczynski, also known as the Unabomber, is given four life sentences plus thirty years in prison for killing three people and injuring twenty-nine with his homemade mail bombs.

August 23—Congress votes to launch an impeachment inquiry against Bill Clinton.

December 19—The House Judiciary Committee approves two articles of impeachment against the president, charging him with lying to a grand jury and obstructing justice by covering up his affair with Monica Lewinsky.

1999

January 7—The Senate begins Clinton's impeachment trial.

February 12—The Senate votes 55-45 against convicting Clinton of the perjury charge against him, and 50-50 on the obstruction of justice charge; the vote puts an end to the possibility of Clinton's impeachment.

April—The United States and its NATO allies begin a bombing campaign in Serbia to protect Muslims in Kosovo; this leads the Serbs to force hundreds of thousands of Kosavars from their homes, creating the worst European refugee crisis since World War II.

April 20—Eighteen-year-old Eric Harris and seventeen-year-old Dylan Klebold kill thirteen students at Columbine High School in Littleton, Colorado, before committing suicide; the killers left at least thirteen pipe bombs in the school and at least eight more bombs inside one of the killers' car; this is the worst school killing in U.S. history to date.

For Further Reading

Tricia Andryszewski, *The Militia Movement in America*. Brookfield, CT: Millbrook, 1997.

David Brin, *The Transparent Society*. Reading, MA: Addison-Wesley, 1998.

James Carville, *And the Horse He Rode in On: The People v. Kenneth Starr*. New York: Simon & Schuster, 1998.

Buffy Childerhose, *From Lilith to Lilith Fair: The Authorized Story*. New York: St. Martin's Griffin, 1998.

Noam Chomsky, *The Chomsky Trilogy: Secrets, Lies and Democracy/The Prosperous Few and the Restless Many/What Uncle Sam Really Wants*. Monroe, ME: Odonian, 1995.

Andrew Cockburn and Patrick Cockburn, *Out of the Ashes: The Resurrection of Saddam Hussein*. New York: HarperCollins, 1999.

Fred Coleman, *The Decline and Fall of the Soviet Empire: Forty Years That Shook the World, from Stalin to Yeltsin*. New York: St. Martin's, 1997.

R.W. Davies, *Soviet History in the Yeltsin Era*. New York: St Martin's, 1997.

Alan M. Dershowitz, *Sexual McCarthyism: Clinton, Starr, and the Emerging Constitutional Crisis*. New York: BasicBooks, 1998.

Zlatko Dizdarevic, *Sarajevo*. New York: Fromm International, 1993.

Elizabeth Drew, *Showdown*. New York: Simon & Schuster, 1996.

Editors of *Rolling Stone*, *Cobain*. New York: Little, Brown, 1994.

Editors of *Time Magazine*, *Desert Storm*. Ed. Otto Friedrich. New York: Little, Brown, 1991.

James Garbarino, *Lost Boys: Why Our Sons Turn Violent and How We Can Save Them*. New York: Free, 1999.

Ross Gelbspan, *The Heat Is On*. Reading, MA: Addison-Wesley, 1997.

Jewelle Taylor Gibbs, *Race and Justice*. San Francisco: Jossey-Bass, 1996.

Al Gore, *Earth in the Balance*. Boston: Houghton Mifflin, 1992.

Philip Gourevitch, *We Wish to Inform You That Tomorrow We Will Be Killed with Our Families: Stories from Rwanda*. New York: Farrar, Straus & Giroux, 1998.

Jim Hightower, *There's Nothing in the Middle of the Road but Yellow Stripes and Dead Armadillos*. New York: Harper-Collins, 1998.

Stanley G. Hilton and Anne-Renee Testa, *Glass Houses: Shocking Profiles of Congressional Sex Scandals and Other Unofficial Misconduct*. New York: St. Martin's, 1998.

Clive Irving, ed., *In Their Name*. New York: Random House, 1995.

Michael Isikoff, *Uncovering Clinton: A Reporter's Story*. New York: Crown, 1999.

Molly Ivins, *You Got to Dance with Them What Brung You: Politics in the Clinton Years*. New York: Vintage Books, 1999.

Russell Jacoby, *The End of Utopia: Politics and Culture in an Age of Apathy*. New York: BasicBooks, 1999.

Wayne Jancik and Steve Roeser, *Noise: Alternative Rock in the '90s*. Kansas City, MO: Andrews McMeel, 1999.

Timothy Judah, *The Serbs, History, Myth, and the Destruction of Yugoslavia*. New Haven, CT: Yale University Press, 1998.

Robert D. Kaplan, *Balkan Ghosts: A Journey Through History*. New York: Vintage Books, 1994.

Howard Kurtz, *Hot Air: All Talk, All the Time*. New York: Times Books, 1996.

David Stuart Lane, Cameron Ross, and Elizabeth Rau Bethel, *The Transition from Communism to Capitalism: Ruling Elites from Gorbachev to Yeltsin*. New York: St. Martin's, 1998.

John R. MacArthur, *Second Front*. New York: Hill and Wang, 1992.

Noel Malcolm, *Kosovo: A Short History*. New York: New York University Press, 1998.

Joyce Milton, *The First Partner: Hillary Rodham Clinton*. New York: William Morrow, 1999.

Carrick Mollenkamp, et al., *The People vs. Big Tobacco*. Princeton, NJ: Bloomberg, 1998.

Michael Moore, *Downsize This!* New York: Crown, 1996.

Kevin Phillips, *Arrogant Capital*. New York: Little, Brown, 1994.

Peter Phillips, *Censored 1997: The News That Didn't Make the News—the Year's Top Twenty-Five Censored News Stories*. New York: Seven Stories, 1997.

Jeremy Rifkin, *The Biotech Century*. New York: Penguin Putnam, 1998.

Scott Ritter, *ENDGAME: Solving the Iraq Problem—Once and For All*. New York: Simon & Schuster, 1999.

Rolling Stone, "The Essential Recordings of the '90s," May 13, 1999.

Mort Rosenblum, *Moments of Revolution*. New York: Stewart, Tobori & Chang, 1990.

Bob Shacochis, *The Immaculate Invasion*. New York: Viking, 1999.

Staff of the *Los Angeles Times*. *Understanding the Riots*. Los Angeles: Los Angeles Times, 1992.

George Stephanopoulos, *All Too Human: A Political Education*. New York: Little, Brown, 1999.

Chuck Sudetic, *Blood and Vengeance: One Family's Story of the War in Bosnia*. New York: Penguin USA, 1999.

Elsie B. Washington, *Uncivil War*. Chicago: Nobel, 1996.

Nick Wise, *Kurt Cobain and Courtney Love: In Their Own Words*. London: Omnibus, 1996.

Alan Wolfe, *One Nation After All*. New York: Viking, 1998.

Index